Comments
of a
Common Man

This book is published in the international English language market and uses the form of English native to the author.

KJM Today
www.kjmtoday.com

First published in the United Kingdom and the United States of America 2017
This edition published in the United Kingdom and the United States of America 2019

ISBN: 9781689961509

Comments of a Common Man

Third Edition

Kevan James

Kevan James is a freelance journalist, author and photographer, specialising in aviation but also has a strong interest in politics, social history and sports. Other books are:

The Posts of Roche Fokke

Heathrow Airport, An Illustrated History

Heathrow. Days Out at the UK's Premier International Airport

Airport. Days and Nights, Terminals and Runways
(with Fay Jordan and Tyler McDowell)

Boyhood. Soccer Skaters Streets and Suchlike

Boysold Trilogy 1 (a novel)

Front Cover –
Towering skyscrapers - the corporate world and big money. Suburbs and the ordinary people (Photo; Author).

Back Cover –
You never know…there may be light at the end of your tunnel too.
If you are very lucky (Photo; Author and modelled by Sam Goldstone Harris)

'Governments don't want a population capable of critical thinking. They want obedient workers just smart enough to run the machines and just dumb enough to passively accept their situation'

George Carlin

Contents

Intro

'Everybody who is somebody was nobody at some point'

Peter McDonagh (1948-2015)
Former Director of Radio, British Forces Broadcasting Service

When I wrote the first edition of this book, almost none of the issues I raised had been spoken of either by politicians or mentioned in mainstream media, at least not specifically. They had however, been discussed at length by ordinary people, me included.

The first edition was published in 2017, a second in 2018 and in the short time since, events have overtaken both editions, hence this version; the third.

The most significant event is that of Brexit, the fall of Theresa May as Prime Minster and the rise of Boris Johnson. Yet there are other aspects that remain unchanged. Some of those very issues – not all, just some - have indeed been raised by those who are privileged to occupy a place the House of Commons, the 'Mother of All Parliaments', as it is sometimes called. Be under no illusions, it is indeed a privilege to be a Member of Parliament, an MP; a privilege that is granted to those members by ordinary people and one that can be taken away by ordinary people. This is one rather vital point that those elected need to be reminded of, and reminded of far too often.

Raised though those issues may have been – and reported in both broadcast and print media - one essential question remains: having mentioned these points, will anything actually be done about them? Or are those comments from those who are supposed to serve us merely window dressing, simply a means to gain good headlines?

One suspects (and with good reason) the latter. It is for that reason that I have updated – again - this book Although still included are many of my original observations, I have enlarged upon them and, as befits the sub-title, I have brought new points of interest into play.

Harold Wilson (1916-95) served twice as Labour Prime Minister during one of the greatest periods of social and industrial change in the twentieth century. During his first period in office, 1964-70, Wilson aimed to modernise Britain by harnessing the 'white heat' of technology. His government abolished capital punishment and liberalised laws on censorship, divorce, abortion and homosexuality. Crucial steps were also taken towards ending discrimination against women and ethnic minorities, and the Open University was created. He became Leader of the Labour Party in 1963 after the sudden death of Hugh Gaitskell, Labour won the following year's General Election with a slim majority of just four seats and Wilson became

Prime Minister for the first time. In the lead up to the election he is supposed to have coined the famous phrase, 'A week is a long time in politics.'

The time between my writing these words and you actually reading them is a lot longer than a week and as we have seen over the past twelve months (up to August 2019), a year is eternity in politics. That however, is the risk I take in producing a book such as this and you buying it – yet another of the risks we take in our lives and as you will see, there are many such risks. If you acquired a copy of the first and second editions, I make no apologies for the text that remains unaltered in this version. Do forgive the repetition however as there may well be those (and I hope many of them) who have not read either of the first two but do have this one. There are however, a few alterations to the original text, some quite subtle, others very noticeable so I do ask fervently that you please read, or read yet once more, quite carefully, lest you miss something.

Otherwise, to begin and as I did before, I am not special. I still have little money and still do not own a house, being a member of 'generation rent' – a generation yet still once more, wrongly considered to be recent. There are in fact, numerous such generations, going back decades and yet more decades and who never did, do not now and will not own their home. Like my Parents.

Both died of cancer and in their seventies, my mother nonetheless being capable of looking after herself until her end but my father less so. Although they had long since divorced, they remained friends but I gave up work to be a full-time carer for dad, wiping his bottom, cleaning him, feeding him and pushing him about in his wheelchair until he finally passed away. A diagnosis of terminal cancer seems often followed by 'You have six months...', but dad being the awkward individual that he was, he lasted a lot longer than that. Being a parental carer is not a path to financial prosperity however and I have been playing catch-up ever since he moved into what follows our earthly life. I would not however, have done anything else – there was never any question of sticking him in some home where he would rot away, possibly mistreated, until death. The net result however is that like many today, I have to accept that (unless this book is bought in huge numbers) I will probably never own my own home; they cost too much.

Like many, I have had to think twice, thrice and sometimes more, before spending what I do have, most of which goes on merely staying alive. In winter, I have had to choose between heating and eating, a premise that has had aspersions cast upon it by some newspaper columnists. I have had to ponder the question of whether or not to go to the launderette and have clean clothes or hand-wash them because I couldn't afford the launderette...and ended up hand-washing so I had the money for food. Like many yet again, I listen to the political elite babbling on and wonder where they live and what planet they come from, since it doesn't seem to be in this country and on the same world as the rest of us. I have had conversations with many like me and those worse off and those better off, both in person and on social media like Facebook, a wonderful tool for keeping in touch and just as with all inventions of humanity, capable of being misused by a minority. So I figured that I would put the results of those conversations into a book - this book.

I claim no expertise however. Neither do I claim to have all the answers. Only that I am fairly ordinary and 'just about managing', as the now former Prime Minster said, and just getting by. Even so, there are those who will think these are the ramblings of a demented nobody (see quote above) or just plain self-opinionated crap - there might even be some who agree with what I have written. Also worth saying is that some of these points (or even all of them) are not new; as far back as 1868, Herbert Spencer raised many of the same issues and they have been raised numerous times since. However, it would be nice to think that rather than simply being dismissed or even merely agreed with, this book will provoke; that it will inform, stimulate debate and possibly even action - at least a little here and there and hopefully in the right way.

It ought to be fairly obvious that this book is primarily aimed at the UK and its occupants but it could also apply to any country anywhere, especially those that consider themselves to be free. If you are one of those who do have that consideration, you may also be one of those who take such freedom for granted – be aware however! The freedoms we once took for granted in the UK are under threat like never before and the source of some of those threats may be something of a surprise, at least to some.

So if this book makes you think, then it has served at least a part of its purpose. After that – it's up to you.

Kevan James
Kent, UK, 2017 - 2019.

1 Risk

'Life is inherently risky. There is only one big risk you should avoid at all costs, and that is the risk of doing nothing'.

Denis Waitley

Freedom is an interesting concept. Can we, as citizens, have real, complete and total freedom? No, we can't. Not if a society is to work - this means we either give up some freedom and have rules or we do not have a society that functions. So we freely give up something. We agree to have rules and we agree to abide by them.

We get the rules from those we as ordinary people, give a job to; we say to anybody who wants this job, 'We will give you the power to make those rules and run our country for us. We give you this job for a limited time only. If we don't like the way you do this job, we'll fire you and give the job to somebody else'. In the United Kingdom, the job of course is that of Member of Parliament, MP for short, and there are currently 650 of them. Whichever political party has the most MPs elected runs our country for us and the leader of the party (and thus becoming Prime Minister) is chosen by those MPs, along with party members, and subsequently chooses his or her Cabinet of Ministers. That, simply put, is the theory of it - and anybody can apply to be an MP. No matter who they are…but anybody can't.

If for example, you broke the law and got sent to prison for twelve months or more, you are not allowed to stand for public office. MP, local Councillor, Mayor, whatever – you are banned, barred and not allowed. Why?

Whether people would vote for and elect somebody with a criminal record is another matter but what if the criminal has done his or her time and been a law-abiding citizen since? What if they have put their past behind them and gone on to be a fully integrated member of society, done good things and paid their taxes? It shouldn't matter that they screwed up before, years ago. If people decide not to give the former law-breaker the job, that's their choice. But it should be the choice of the former law-breaker to ask for the job. Democracy doesn't work very well if anybody is excluded from the most vital part of it; the part that says 'you' (as in anybody) can take part in the debate, join the discussion and be one of those who make the rules. One could say that there is a risk in giving the job to somebody who committed a crime at some point – but just because the candidate hasn't committed a crime doesn't mean to say they won't once they have their sticky paws anywhere near the levers of power. There are after all, plenty who have done just that. So there is a risk - and that's the part about freedom that people don't get. Freedom carries with it risk:

    The risk that we might get blown up.
    The risk that we might be run over by a drunk driver.
    The risk that we might be robbed.
    The risk that we might, as children, be molested.
    The risk that…

There are many - but we either accept those risks or we are not free.

You cannot legislate for everything. The state – its rule-makers, the ones we give the job to – cannot micro-manage the society it is supposed to serve. If it does, or tries to, society is not free and becomes oppressed. Winston Churchill once said, 'The more Laws there are, the more likely people are to break them.'

This is where we are today; and like sheep, we simply accept what we are spoon-fed by our Government. More laws compelling us not to do something (not saying what we *can* do…just what we can't). We have become an oppressed people - we have become sheeple.

'Everything is great! The Government has my best interests in mind!'

Sheeple – people who unquestioningly accept as true whatever their, often self-appointed, leaders say or people who adopt 'popular' opinion (usually based on screaming headlines and sensationalist articles in newspapers) as their own without scrutiny; people who don't think for themselves.

Where does this end? Are we, now, today, seeing the death throes of real freedom? Or has it gone already?

Will we, one day soon, wake up at the time we are told to; eat the breakfast that we are told to eat; go to work using the method of public transport we are told to since we're not allowed to have our own cars; do the job that we are told to; have the lunch we are told to at the time we are told to; go back to the same job we are given by the state before ending our day at the time we are told to; returning to the home we are told to live in by the state; doing the leisure activity we are told to have and for the amount of time we are told to; before eating the last meal of the day we are told eat; watching the TV we are told to; going to bed when we are told to; not having sex when we both feel horny and want to because its forbidden except when the state decrees which night we are allowed to do it…before going to sleep for the regulated amount of time and then repeating this procedure the next day and every day of every week of every year of every decade of life and for the entire duration of it.

Mr. and Mrs. Jones! Stop! Tonight is not your night for officially sanctioned copulation! Mr. Jones! Withdraw immediately and take your anti-erection tablet! You are not permitted to have sex until next month on Thursday the twelfth!"

Risk

The booming voice echoes from the state home communication system, demanding an instant end to the unmentionable act, viewed via the state home surveillance system by some anonymous state official whose state-empowered task it is to supervise Mr. and Mrs. Jones.

Once we have had our regulated act of love and produced the regulated one child permitted as there is no room to have more than one, it will be removed from us at birth and taken to a secure state education establishment where it will be taught how to live properly and grow up free of any danger of being abused by an adult – when your child reaches eighteen and is then an adult he or she will be sent back to you. This is how the state education system will work because child protection is paramount and *all* adults are abusers.

Without exception - including the new one who just got sent home. This is how we will live. Until we reach the age at which we are no longer considered to be a useful member of society as we are too old and infirm and are thus euthanized to make room for somebody else. In the Movie *Logan's Run* the age of state killing is thirty years of age. Get to thirty and that's your lot; there is not enough food, there are not enough places for people to live so at thirty, the state euthanizes you as it doesn't want old people around.

Don't be daft! It will never happen.

It already is. Granted in a less extreme form – so far – but the thin end of these particular wedges have already been inserted, and rather subtly in most cases, into our lives. The state has started telling us what to eat, when and how much. The state has already started telling people what kind of home they are allowed to live in and all too frequently, tells us what kind of life we must lead

Logan's Run is coming - and it's coming right around the corner at you.

Something else the state does already is steal children from their parents for any reason and often the slightest perception of there being a reason, however flimsy it might be. Yes, there are too many occasions when somebody messes up and a child dies. But children have always died, and too often at the hands of those who are supposed to love and protect them - parents mess up more than most. There are too many parents who have either forgotten how to love and protect their young or who have never been taught how to properly - which doesn't say much for *their* parents either. With each generation, the ability to raise children has been eroded, mostly however by the state and its agents and by a lack of people willing to say, 'Get out of our lives State! You are not our masters, we are yours. We are a free people and that includes the freedom to screw our lives up and make mistakes.'

Which means people, including children, occasionally will die.

Freedom means risk.

But the state continues to impose its will more and more and the sheeple say and do nothing. You want to be risk-free. Sorry, life isn't like that. It has risk and if you want to be truly free then accept that risk. Or you will not be free.

Want another example? In March 2017, the US Department of Homeland Security decreed that laptops, I-Pads and other electronic equipment over a certain size will not be allowed to be carried in the aircraft cabin with you on board flights from six countries, all in the mid-east. Such equipment must now be checked in and placed in the aircraft hold with other checked-in baggage. That size limit includes cameras. Naturally, with almost immediate acquiescence, the British Government followed suit. What this meant is that if travelling from, say, Singapore to the UK and changing flights at Istanbul, one can take a camera on the Singapore-Istanbul leg, but not from Istanbul to London.

The reason for this is the fear of such equipment being used as bombs. However, one can still take one's mobile phone on board. So…since mobile phones can (and have) been used to trigger bombs…why are they still allowed? Simply check in your laptop bomb, take off and at the time of your choosing, take out your mobile and everybody goes to meet their maker.

One of my magazine editors declared airports in the six countries, and their airlines, off-limits and said that he has no intention of checking in his high-value camera equipment, all of which fits into a regulation-sized carry on bag, the same sentiment being expressed in numerous Facebook posts. I added my own comments and made the point that it is only a matter of time before it's is extended to *all* flights.

Monday 27 March 2017, just over a week later; then UK Home Secretary Amber Rudd suggested that such an extension may happen…so kiss goodbye to more of your precious freedom and the ability to record your holiday from start to finish (flight out and flight back) or work on board and my camera gear, which, like yours, will be highly liable to theft or damage if checked in on ANY flight, anywhere, ain't going in no cargo hold, to be nicked or thrown around by some bag handler, videos of the same having been posted on Facebook and Youtube, much to everybody's annoyance.

It seems to me that pre-flight security checks should be capable of ascertaining if a laptop or camera has explosives hidden inside but as always these days, those with power would rather take the easier path and oppress the freedom of the individual.

Fear rules! So the bad guys are winning and yet again, the risk that goes with freedom is nullified - as is freedom itself.

The restrictions mentioned above were subsequently relaxed, at least a little, but even though the reason for their being introduced to begin with might have been sound enough, like many such examples, the delivery and thus the effect on ordinary lives, was a perfect example of the Law of Unintended Consequences. Like many similar instances, such restrictions are easily introduced and even though they may be withdrawn (for a time) it doesn't take much for them to be brought back into use and there are many that do remain in force no matter what. When that happens – as it has and does all too often – the future can be rather more worrisome.

This possible scenario is one that should be of some concern:

> Cuthbert Jones-Smyth reached into his pocket, took out his identity card and hung it around his neck using the officially issued lanyard. He always did when travelling, whether by bus, air (even though that was severely restricted in today's world) or, as now, by train. Nobody of course, had cars anymore. They had been banned a while back, except of course, for use by government officials and the state security service. He looked back at the lengthy queues at the bus stops outside the station. It always took a while to get on a bus now; firstly one had to go through the security check before actually getting to the stop itself and then there was the wait for a bus to actually arrive. At least he would be travelling today since the train crews were not on strike, although inevitably, they were running late. He glanced up at the rolling news screens on the station concourse – an announcement was due from the President, broadcast by the single state-run TV and radio station that now existed. That's why the trains were late; everything stopped when the President made one of his announcements. He looked around; everybody had their eyes fixed on the screen as the face of President Corbyn appeared.
>
> "My fellow citizens," he said smoothly, his voice echoing slightly around the concourse. "Today is yet another great day in our country's history. As you know, since I became President, we have revolutionised the way in which we do things. Our policies of state control over everything, including the automation of almost every job, has meant wonderful Citizens Dividend payments to you all so that you can enjoy your daily lives…"
>
> Cuthbert risked a quick look at the station shops, all permanently closed now, as they had been for a long time. Only the state-run news store was open. His gaze returned to the big screen as President Corbyn continued.
>
> "I have dedicated my life to the service of you all and I am pleased to say that our country is the socialist utopia we

promised you, that *your* safety has been maintained..." Out of the corner of his eye, Cuthbert noticed the dark-shirted, uniformed security service officers hustling away a woman who had been caught not watching and listening to the President. She would be taken...somewhere.

Nobody knew where. Or if she would ever be seen again. Probably not. He kept his face looking at the screen as President Corbyn went on.

"As you know, in order to protect you and for you to be safe, I was forced to cancel the general elections that were due to be held on the past two occasions due to security fears. I regret to have to tell you that I am obliged to do the same now and this year's general election will not be held as we have not yet defeated the enemies of the state. The internet and social media will remain closed for the same reason. Today however, marks a new dawn in the history of the Republic of England. I have done my part and its time for me to step down and make way for my chosen successor. I have anointed my Vice-President and Chancellor, John McDonnell, to take over from me and he will assume the position of President one month from today. I will broadcast to you again a little closer to the time, with John at my side, as he has been since we swept to power all those wonderful years ago and transformed our country. Thank you."

Cuthbert sighed. No surprises there then. Not for the first time, he wondered if it really was Corbyn since nobody had actually seen him for years. Mind you, the same applied to McDonnell. Today's technology meant it would be easy to produce a totally convincing computer-generated version of the President for these broadcasts. Even more so since the state had taken all aspects of that technology under its direct control – get caught with it yourself, at home or elsewhere and that was you swallowed into the dark maw of the state, never to be seen again. He headed towards the security channels, pausing by a map of the country. Well, at least he wasn't going far, even if it did take six hours these days to take the train from London to Northampton. At the far north, the bright blue outline of the European Province of Scotland stood out. To the west, the red of the European Region of Wales. Further west, across the sea, the green of the United Irish Republic, both again outlined in the dark blue of their European provincial status. He took his place in the queue at security and smiled at the security officer doing spot checks on the people waiting.

Risk

"Papers!" barked the officer as he reached Cuthbert, who held out his ID card on its lanyard. The officer snapped to attention. "Sir! Please…come with me, *you* don't have to wait with the rest."

"I know," replied Cuthbert. "But I prefer to, it helps me in my work since I have to deal with ordinary people."

The security officer leaned forward slightly, his voice lowered. "I really must insist Sir. Its not acceptable for a senior Government official to be mixed in…" he looked at the queue with obvious distaste. "…with ordinary people like this."

"Is that an instruction, Officer?" asked Cuthbert.

"Well, I wouldn't put it quite like that, Sir," replied the officer. "But I have my orders."

Cuthbert sighed again. "Oh well. I wouldn't want you to get into trouble so lead on then."

The officer smiled. "Excellent Sir. I'll have you on the train very quickly."

"What about these people?"

The officer shrugged indifferently. "Some will get on, some won't."

They approached the expansive security check booth. The officer running it looked closely at Cuthbert's ID and checked his name was on the list of those supposed to be travelling and with approval to do so.

"Yes, you are here," he said, almost in monotone. "I see you booked nice and early. Very wise Sir. I see also you are travelling to see your Mother?"

Cuthbert nodded. "Yes, she will be fifty years old next week so this is the last chance I will have to see her before she goes for state euthanasia. I need to say goodbye."

"My sympathies Sir. Still, as loyal citizens we'll all be going there. We can't have old people clogging up the health system, using up scarce food supplies or taking up valuable living space, can we Sir?"

"Indeed not, Officer."

The first officer then indicated the VIP entry. "Come along then Sir, I'll escort you to your seat on the train. Might be a while before it goes though. Still, at least you can wait comfortably."

"Thank you," replied Cuthbert. He took a swift look back at the waiting queue. Most looked careworn and underfed. Resigned to doing what they were told to do. They looked old. As the officer with the list had implied, some of them looked like they were getting close to fifty. Maybe it was just the way their lives were these days.

It made them look older. Nobody actually got old now though.

Unless you were the President, that is.

The above is of course, fiction.

It couldn't possibly happen here!

Perhaps not – but then again, consider a speech made by the head of Ofsted, Amanda Spielman, in June 2018, in which she said, 'Children should be encouraged to play on park equipment because risk is a part of a proper childhood'. She urged nursery staff not to 'obsess too much about health and safety because it inhibits play and a child's natural development'. Her point was that nurseries, schools and local authorities have removed traditional children's play equipment and even trees from playgrounds because they put kids at risk from falling or slipping. Spielman went on to say, 'Of course we expect you to take risk seriously and to supervise children properly. But equally…some level of risk is part of a proper childhood. And without it, we stifle children's natural inquisitiveness and their opportunities to learn.'

Yet in the UK, there are innumerable parents of equally innumerable children who have *already been* through a system in which risk is either eliminated or strenuous attempts made to eliminate it, and who are now bringing up their children to be afraid of everything. Not to be aware and to take care – just to be afraid. Of everything.

To eliminate risk can only be done through complete and total control by those in a position to exercise that control. Which means you must be told what to do, when to do it, how to do it and most of all, not to do it at all – whatever 'it' might be.

'It' is forbidden and is so 'for your safety'.

This is also part of the methodology employed by the far left in order to gain complete control over everyone's lives; now think of the behaviour of some of those who support Jeremy Corbyn and take a good, long, hard look at many of the opinions and comments of John McDonnell – and when you get to it, read the later chapter on both and those behind them, as well as the pronouncements and actions of the political elite.

So I say for the second time - the state continues to impose its will more and more and the sheeple say and do nothing. You want to be risk-free. Sorry, life isn't like that. It has risk and if you want to be truly free then accept that risk. Or you will not be free.

·

2 Broken

'History, despite its wrenching pain, cannot be unlived, but if faced with courage, need not be lived again'.

Maya Angelou

People often witter on about how this or that is wrong, saying something like, 'They should do something about that...'

Who is, or are, 'they'? In and around your local town, usually 'they' means the local council (or city authority). At national level, it's the Government. The truth of it is neither is really responsible for whatever it is that is wrong.

You are.

Yes, you – the ordinary citizen; the common man and woman. You elect people to serve on your local council and you elect them to employ people to serve your needs, which include keeping the street lights on, filling potholes in those streets and collecting your rubbish each week (yes – each and every week), amongst other things. To fund it, you pay your local council tax. To fund running the country, you pay your national income tax (from which also comes extra cash for local services via Government).

Put another way, *you* pay them to do the job *you* have given them.

Assuming you do pay your taxes and go and vote at elections, that makes you the boss. Not the local councillor or council employee. They are not in charge, you are. They are not your masters, you are theirs. A point which also applies to the Government; you elect them, you give somebody a job as your Member of Parliament, they employ civil servants to serve your needs and run your country for you. Even the Prime Minister is responsible to each and every citizen. You...are the Prime Minister's boss.

Just as you are the boss of your local council. Out of your taxes come the very often stratospheric salaries paid to those who run things. These salaries put council chiefs on a par with the CEOs of big, privately-owned and international companies; but those CEOs, for the most part, generate big amounts of money for their companies and their shareholders. At one time, the council's head officer was called the Town Clerk; today, he or she is indeed given the title Chief Executive Officer, with that matching income.

Yet all they do is spend your hard-earned money, money taken by law from you. Your local council – and its employees, including its head, whatever their title - is meant to deal with waste disposal, maintain the roads and street lights, parks and leisure facilities, care services and other necessary things. Instead, they seem to introduce more ways to spend your money *and without* providing the services you pay for.

So why have you fallen into the habit of meekly accepting everything they say and putting up with unlit, pot-holed roads, uncollected garbage, failing schools and a myriad of other things, which your local employees tell you are always, *always* due to the 'savage cuts' imposed by the Government (something that has been said for most of my life by the way)? Why are you finding yourselves wondering how many rats are going to be attracted to your increasingly un-emptied bins since the council dictated to you that those bins will now only be emptied just once a fortnight? Oh…wait…make that once every three weeks…no…no….once a month… You may well moan to each other but what are you, as citizens and as the ones who are really in charge, doing about it? Actually, not very much – except whine about it. I do not propose armed insurrection or mass violence, neither do I propose action to 'bring down this wicked government' (unlike some recently), at least not until a valid general election. So why are you like you are today?

To find out one has to go back in history, look at it, learn from it, and understand it.

On Tuesday October 29, 2013, in an article for the Daily Mail newspaper, Yasmin Alibhai-Brown wrote that the now-retired TV interviewer Jeremy Paxman couldn't understand why people drop litter and commented further that she found the attitude displayed by people who do just as baffling as Paxman himself did.

On page 11 of the same edition, the Mail carried a report of a forty-four-year-old man, beaten and burned to death by two individuals, both of whom were aged twenty-four, seemingly egged on by the lynch mob mentality of those around them, who thought he was a paedophile, since he had apparently been arrested by the police for taking photographs of children. It transpired that that their innocent victim had been photographing local youths vandalising his garden, with the intent of handing the photos to the police and local council.

By the way, it's not illegal in the UK and is not therefore an arrestable offence or an offence of any kind, to take photographs of children (or of anybody else).

The Daily Mail ran an admirable campaign for dignity for the elderly and yet again in the same edition – October 29 – reported on a review into standards of care, jointly written by Ann Clwyd MP, whose husband was unfortunate enough to need a stay in hospital, where he died 'like a battery hen' as a result of the neglect now all too common in UK hospitals. In her article, Alibhai-Brown asked 'why are so many of us casting aside all semblance of social responsibility along with our empty cans, sweet wrappers and crisp bags?'

Broken

The answer is to be found decades ago.

Although there have been numerous theories aired as to the ills of our technologically-advanced modern-day society, some revolving around a few of those advances, none delve back into our history as a nation, and only by doing so and understanding our history will we stand any chance of recovering that social responsibility, not just in terms of littering but in so many other areas of our daily life.

One thing never admitted to is that we British are by nature, a violent people, which is why we are so good at winning wars. Opinions may vary as to our success in Afghanistan and Iraq but there is no doubting that when we enter an armed conflict by ourselves, free of any consideration of others, the record of our armed services is second to none. Could any other nation have sent a task force halfway around the world, all the way to the Falkland Islands, to take on a much bigger opponent based close by, and won? Could any other nation have successfully fought off a vastly superior force as the tiny garrison at Rorke's Drift did against 4,000 Zulu warriors? Yes, we have lost, occasionally, and yes, other countries have their own examples of great heroism and fighting capability but none has such a consistent record as the British.

We are also inclined to like alcohol, often to excess. Where else in the world could one find small villages, some with only one street, yet two (or more) pubs? The world of Charles Dickens was full of violent drunken behaviour. When I moved to my present address almost two decades ago within five minutes walk of my home there were no less than five pubs, one bar and one working men's club. Eight places licensed to serve alcoholic beverages. That same scenario is, or was, repeated the length and breadth of the country. Granted many of those have now closed (including all five pubs and the bar near me), mostly for financial reasons and significantly since the Labour Party's smoking ban, but every corner shop and every supermarket also sells alcohol and does so in huge quantities.

So we like a fight. We like a few pints. We always have. Yet for all the ready availability and opportunities of these things, there was still a sense of social responsibility to be found in all walks of British life. So what happened and when?

Like every society, Britain developed in a way that, with some hiccups, worked. The industrial revolution saw tiny villages become towns, and small towns become great cities. It wasn't perfect, far from it in fact, but it did work. Britain sent people all over the world and the inventiveness and imagination of those people saw great advances made, both abroad and within the UK itself. By the time of World War One, Britain was truly a great nation, albeit an imperfect one. That began to change after the end of World War Two. By this time, people had started to tire of being sent to some far corner of the world, and the seeds of discontent were beginning to sprout. One inevitable result of global conflict, with two barely twenty years apart, was that technological advances tend to speed up, a result of necessity to defeat the enemy – and we won, both times. Yet Britain in the late 1940s and early 1950s was still struggling to overcome the effects of war. The country was broke. As young people grew older, the memories of those two world wars were still fresh. History – real history - was taught in schools and a generation was aware that the old order had failed and prosperity was still a dream for most people. Those technological advances were not filtering down to everybody (there were still plenty of pubs to be found though).

As the 1950s progressed, those who were in their teens ten years earlier were now young adults and gaining influence, not just in their own lives but in the lives of others too. They didn't want what their parents had. They didn't want the way of life that so many had become accustomed to. They wanted change - and they made change happen. By the middle of the 1960s, they now had almost-grown children themselves, all of whom were entering adulthood and this new wave of young people had the freedom to express themselves in ways that their grandparents never dreamt possible. Not that the grandparents approved of the new way. They went to the pub just as they always had, and grumbled that kids today had no idea of the sacrifices made in their day - and they were right.

Somewhere in the late 1950s and throughout the 1960s, we as a nation, lost sight of many of the responsibilities that had welded the country together. We stopped teaching our children right from wrong. We stopped teaching history. As the children of that era became adults and had children themselves, the disparity between working for what you want and simply demanding it became ever greater. We stopped doing certain things. In the 1970s and early 1980s, we took away street litterbins because the IRA kept putting bombs in them; but we never taught people to respond accordingly. So they just dropped their rubbish where they stood. That was passed on so even though bins have now reappeared, there are generations, some now parents themselves, who have never used them. They simply don't know what a street litterbin is for.

Today we are paying the price for being so dismissive of the old ways. Some of today's children and young people (not all but a significant number) have no conception of the things that brought the social responsibility that Yasmin Alibhai-Brown wrote of - they have never been taught them. The old ways were not perfect and things did indeed need to change. But the result of *how* that change happened is what we see in hospitals today; nurses that regard the old as a nuisance; university students on a drunken night out urinating on a war memorial because they have no idea what the memorial means; feral school-age children who vandalise someone's garden because it's fun; innocent men brutally killed by a baying mob who have never been taught to think first; feckless single mothers who believe that the state should support their multi-child households.

Career politicians…who have never had a real job, have no idea of the lives of the ordinary average person, have never lived through a war and have never seen at first hand the devastating consequences of their desire to strut the world stage.

The responsibility for society today lies with the Parents, Grandparents and Great-grandparents of yesterday.

A perfect example of poor parenting today comes from Amanda Spielman (mentioned in the last chapter). As head of Ofsted, Spielman warned that too many children today are starting their first year at school at four and five years old, unable to speak properly (for their age obviously), unable to dress themselves and even unable to use the toilet properly because – they haven't been taught these first basic steps of life by their parents. Some children of this age have even been sent to their first year of education still wearing nappies… A recent survey of teachers by the Centre for Social Justice found that a fifth of them spent some thirty minutes a week toilet-training children and sixty per cent of teachers rated pupil's toilet hygiene as poor.

So why are parents not doing it? Because…*their* parents didn't teach them how to raise the grandchildren. There are also other factors at work here; one set of parents (on comfortable salaries) in Surrey advertised for a £50-an-hour professional potty trainer to get their three-year-old daughter out of nappies; The mother, aged thirty-six, was quoted as saying that as she and her partner work full-time in demanding jobs they 'simply do not have the time to do so'.

Take a bus ride in your local area and there is a very good chance you will see parents of young children transfixed by their mobile phones and not looking after their kids. There is an equal chance that those same parents will behave in the same or a very similar way at home, rather than actually giving their own children the start in basic life skills that they need. This same comment has been made by Melanie Pilcher, Policy and Standards Manager at the Pre-School Learning Alliance, who warned that literacy levels were affected by parents who spend too much time online.

Sorry, but if you are going to have children, time is no excuse. You make time - and that includes *not* having the kind of job that pays you enough to pay somebody else to do your job as a parent. It also begs the question; who taught the Surrey mother to use the toilet? Obvious answer – her parents. Yet why did they not finish the job and teach her how to bring up their grandchildren? Including potty training. Why did the parents of the phone-fixated not teach their children to spend time with the grandchildren? It is not only a question of poorly-brought up parents but also a question of the plain selfish.

You may of course, be somebody who is a parent of more mature years, or even a grandparent, and find my comments about parents, grandparents and great-grandparents being responsible for the ills of today a little wide of the mark. Consider therefore, the case of Helen Butcher, of Ulverston, in Cumbria.

In June 2017, Butcher boarded a holiday jet bound for the Greek island of Kos. In July 2018, having waited a year for the case to come to court, she was jailed for six months for her drunken mid-air rampage during the flight. Whilst the aircraft was *en-route*, Butcher assaulted two members of the cabin crew, upset other passengers with her foul-mouthed (and loud) language, and was arrested by Greek police immediately on landing. What she was not however, was an air-headed young twenty-something on a bender.

Helen Butcher was fifty-one at the time and was with her daughter.

Fifty-one? *Fifty-one?* One might expect a mature lady, and a parent, to be of age to set a good example. It seems not. Middle-aged hooliganism and one of the best examples of a bad example. The mind may well boggle yet Helen Butcher is far from unique.

So what do we do about it? *Can* we do anything about it? Is it possible to see a day in the future when older members of our society are valued and respected, despite the laxity of the past? When anybody who needs medical care is looked after and not left in some hospital corridor to die? A day when children and young people will grow up having some respect for themselves and their surroundings, along with their neighbours? Anything is possible. There may be a gradual change coming from some the young. Not all by any manner of means but just as their forefathers did over sixty years ago, they want change. They don't want the world that they live in today to be the world they inherit tomorrow; and they have one huge advantage over their predecessors – the internet. Provided of course, that the state has not either restricted your access to it or cut it off entirely, using terrorism or child protection (or both) as the reasons.

For all its undoubted drawbacks, the World Wide Web is essentially a wonderful thing and has given those who use it properly opportunities to see and gain experiences that their parents never had and they are more aware of what is going on in the world than they are often given credit for. This was graphically demonstrated in the UK General Election of 2017 (see later) and the old - very old - adage of children being seen and not heard is long gone and many of today's young people, despite the misdemeanours of far too many of their peers, and the poor example of their parents, grandparents and great-grandparents, have a voice and are either using it or are prepared to use it. It's going to be hard to overcome

Broken

decades of neglect and there remain far too many who will slide into the bad habits of their predecessors. Perhaps it will take another twenty years or more for these new seeds to bear fruit. It will help enormously if enough of those who either were in power or are in power (holding the job *you* gave them) will admit they got things wrong – so far there is little sign of that. If however the will is there, there is hope. So the answer to Yasmin Alibhai-Brown's question lies in the history books. Go look it all up. Then teach your children – if you haven't already – and your grandchildren that there is a difference between right and wrong, there is a better way to behave and that one day, they too will be old. *They too*…will be old. Then ask them what kind of world they want to live in and grow older in.

Does anybody remember former Prime Minister David Cameron making comments about Britain being broken and being generally derided for saying so, with most commentary suggesting nobody knew what he was on about?

Let me give an example – leaving aside the likes of Helen Butcher, and there are many of them - I use my local library frequently (use them or lose them…). As I stood outside one day recently, two young girls, mid-teens I guess, emerged, still wearing school uniform - the school day had not long ended at the time - and both drinking cola from McDonald's paper cups. One almost finished hers and threw the cup on the ground, with lid and straw, several feet in front of her. The second girl did the same moments later. Not merely dropped - threw. I see this kind of uncaring, unthinking attitude a lot, and not just from those in their teens. I saw something similar at my local railway station around thirteen or fourteen years ago, that time from a boy again in his mid-teens; well over a decade on, he might be a parent now. It simply didn't occur to any of the three to find a bin....and there's the rub; that same attitude is displayed by those much older than this trio, including those old enough to be *their* parents. They are a minority. Probably - but a significant minority, which is why our streets are so dirty. Not just streets in towns and cities but roadsides generally along with railway embankments, rivers and other places. Liberal amounts of discarded plastic and other waste material cover vast areas of the UK - it is a country strewn with litter. Campaigns to clear the country of rubbish thrown thoughtlessly away are admirable and praiseworthy but miss one essential point; why is that rubbish lying about to begin with? Who put it there?

You did.

If not you, then your children. Your relatives and your friends. At the very least, somebody just like you merely dumped it instead of disposing of it properly and insisting, demanding, that local councils do the job that you pay them for.

The UK is not alone in its profligacy or its wasteful habits but compare the streets here to those in some other countries.
Broken Britain? It still is.

■

3 Political Candidacy

*'We are fast approaching the stage of the ultimate inversion: the stage
where the government is free to do anything it pleases, while the citizens
may act only by permission; which is the stage of the darkest periods of
human history – the rule by brute force*

Ayn Rand

'So you want to be a politician? Tell me, what are your
qualifications?

'I'm twenty-four, just out of University, where I studied Politics
and I've spent a year working as an advisor for a sitting MP'

'Sorry, not acceptable – Next!...so you want to be a politician? Tell
me, what are your qualifications?'

'I'm nineteen and I'm young 'n' funky and want to change things.'

'Sorry, not acceptable – Next!...so you want to be a politician? Tell
me, what are your qualifications?'

'Like, I'm sixteen, droppin' ahtta da furver eddycashun wut I'm
forced to 'ave and I'm like, younger 'n' funkier 'n wut that last one
was. An' I wanna vote an' all'.

'Sorry, not acceptable – Next!...so you want to be a politician? Tell
me, what are your qualifications?'

'I'm thirty-five, I'm still young 'n' funky and I was an MP for ten
years in my previous constituency until I lost my seat at the last
election, where I became an MP after I left University where I
studied politics'.

'Ever done anything else?'

'Anything else? I don't follow…'

'What else have you done apart from be a career politician?'

'Um….well….nothing.'

'Sorry, not acceptable – Next!...so you want to be a politician? Tell
me, what are your qualifications?'

'I'm twenty-nine and I'm a lawyer…'

'Sorry, not acceptable – Next!...so you want to be a politician? Tell
me, what are your qualifications?'

'I'm a thirty-year old rich posh boy with inherited millions and I
want it so I'm having it. I'm entitled.'

'Sorry, not acceptable – Next!...so you want to be a politician? Tell
me, what are your qualifications?'

'I'm fifty-nine, and I started working on the railways when I left
school at sixteen, got a mortgage and bought my own house, then
started my own business but went bankrupt under the Conservatives

in the 1980s when they kept putting up interest rates and couldn't afford the mortgage anymore so lost my home, but I recovered and carried on working before giving up work to be a full-time carer for my father, who was dying of cancer. After he died, I went back to work, started another business and although I have never made a lot of money, I earned enough to live on, pay my bills, including my taxes. I've now passed the business on to my partner as I would like to go into politics and I would very much like to use my life experience, listen to people and to serve my constituents if I am elected'.

'Okay…the job is yours. When can you start?'

Who would you give the job to?

That last example isn't me by the way (although there are similarities) and lest one thinks I am being a little contradictory by suggesting that certain people should be excluded from becoming politicians and making the rules the rest of us have to abide by, this is not so; all of the above are free to ask for the job. Just as those to whom they address the question are free to turn them down and there is nothing to stop any of them coming back to ask again later in their lives.

Why do people want to become Members of Parliament? Why, given the media scrutiny that some members come under, particularly those who rise up the pecking order and become Ministers of State, would anybody voluntarily put themselves forward?

Almost all will say something along the lines of, 'I want to make a difference', or, 'I want to put something into Society'. Words to that effect anyway. Yet most MPs are, despite the comment above regarding media scrutiny, fairly anonymous and unknown outside the constituency they represent. Even within them, some people are hard-pressed to name their MP. Can you name yours? Many can't.

Keeping that last point in mind, let's look at what should be known to everybody. MPs are divided into two distinct groups; back benchers, who are the unknown ones, and front benchers, the ones who have a Government job, the highest of which is obviously Prime Minister. There are numerous government jobs, some of which are still relatively obscure and rarely see any media attention and for the most part, the ones we hear about and see on TV are the Ministers of State like the Chancellor of the Exchequer who spends your taxes, the Home Secretary who is responsible for what happens in the UK, the Foreign Secretary who deals with the UK's affairs outside the country's borders. All are still MPs and the basic annual salary for an MP (from 1 April 2019) is £79,468. MPs also receive expenses to cover the costs of running an office, employing staff, having somewhere to live in London and in their constituency, and travelling between

Parliament and that constituency. On top of this, for those that become one, they also get a salary for being a Minister, which may be why some MPs seem so keen on climbing the greasy pole (and doesn't say much for their moral compass or their stated desire to put something into society).

For those who may be unaware, the so-called 'Four Great Offices of State' are those mentioned above, the Prime Minister being the first, for obvious reasons. The next is Chancellor of the Exchequer, followed by the Home Secretary and the Foreign Secretary. Traditionally, those who became Prime Minister will have held at least one of the other three posts. That tradition however, has been broken a number of times, most notably by David Cameron and more recently Jeremy Corbyn, as Leader of the Opposition and who would become Prime Minister if Labour win a general election while he is leader, with both having been criticised for lacking the experience that comes with holding such high office.

Yet that experience can be a double-edged sword. One of David Cameron's selling points was that he was untarnished by having been an MP for a very long before declaring his willingness to stand as Conservative Party Leader. He was fresh and new. One of his opponents in that contest was Kenneth Clarke. Clarke had been Chancellor and an MP for many years before he stood for the leadership. Yet Cameron won – why did Clarke lose? He lost because of that time already spent in parliament. He was not generally thought of as having been a bad Chancellor; actually the reverse – when Tony Blair's New Labour won the 1997 General Election, Clarke left the incoming Government a golden legacy of an economy in very good shape.

What Labour did with it was another story but Kenneth Clarke was seen as one of the 'old guard', one of those who had spent time plotting and planning to become Prime Minister. In other words serving his own interests, rather than those of his constituents and of the country. Whether that was true or not only Clarke himself knows but such a charge can certainly be made of some MPs.

MPs are, however, like everybody else. Most do not rise up a career path, getting the extra cash such a rise brings. Most remain on the back benches and serve their constituents. It's probably fair to say that some of them do serve well and are good MPs, easy to get in touch with and always doing their best to help those they were elected by. Some of the things MPs are asked to help with are things that matter greatly to those affected, like a problem with welfare benefits (one of the most common) or getting the NHS to stir itself and do the job it is supposed to. Ordinary, everyday and sometimes mundane things, that never come near the eyes and ears of a Government Minister.

Yet even the Prime Minister is still a constituency representative, a

Member of Parliament, still supposed to represent people in that constituency, still supposed to hold a regular surgery and help when asked to do so. Today however, it has become increasingly difficult for some to even have written contact with their MP, let alone see them to ask for help with something. In some respects this is actually understandable and especially so since the murder of Jo Cox, who had become well-known to her constituents as being easily accessible, easy to get in touch with. Sometime before Jo Cox's passing, another MP was stabbed by someone at his surgery. Fortunately he survived, but the result is that MPs are becoming more detached from those they are supposed to serve.

It is one of the risks of having the system we have; if you want to be an MP, it means being available to your constituents and there may be a small number of them that might want to do you some harm. If you don't want to run that risk, don't be an MP. That said, we as a society have a genuine and real responsibility to protect those we elect – dead MPs are of no use to anybody and the threat of violence faced today is as real for an MP as it is for everybody. Keeping the balance between accessibility and security is a tricky task however, and the harder it is to get in touch with one's MP, the less accountable he or she will be.

How does one get to be an MP? It is supposed to be fairly straightforward; join the local branch of the political party of your choice and put your name forward for possible selection. Then attend the meetings and interviews required and if successful, you become the candidate when the next general election comes along.

In truth it can be a little more complicated. The Conservatives some years ago introduced an official list of those approved to become candidates, rather than leave it to the local branch to select somebody. To get on that list meant attending an interview at the party's headquarters and passing it. The thinking behind this was that some local selections had proved to be a little random and a more uniform style was needed. This may have had 'some' merit but the result was that candidates became more bland, more dull and less reflective of the area they were supposed to represent.

The waters become more muddied - and this applies to all parties and goes back decades - when an MP from one part of the country lost their seat at a general election, then re-appeared four or five years later standing in another constituency at the other end of the country, the local branch having been 'encouraged' to select them by party high-ups. It becomes even more blurred when having been unsuccessful in one place, those wanting to be MPs tout themselves around the country, seeking selection in a number of constituencies (and having the money to tout themselves with). This is made even worse by the same party high-ups who more or less impose their own preferred candidate somewhere by encouraging very young wannabe politicians in their early twenties to stand in a constituency they have no hope of winning so they can gain campaign experience before being parachuted into a safe seat the next time around.

Such youthful candidates can also generally be relied on to toe the party line and do what they are told by more senior party officials.

Going back specifically to the Conservatives again, the list idea became even more exclusive when, under David Cameron, two lists were devised, the 'A' list and the 'B' list; the 'A' list was comprised of those Cameron thought politically desirable, primarily women and those from minority groups, the 'B' list made up of those who were expendable, who could be fielded in seats that were safe Labour constituencies and who didn't matter if they were unsuccessful. The principle arose as a result of a Labour initiative under Tony Blair, in which all-women candidate lists were drawn up and imposed on constituencies, thus barring men. As I have already said, democracy doesn't work very well if anybody is excluded from it.

Although the idea of trying to have candidates from all walks of life is a good one, like so many good ideas, when left in the hands of the few it amounts keeping the pool of MPs to a select number and in effect, stopping the ordinary person from getting anywhere close to Parliament, especially those actually from the area they live and work in.

Perhaps it is time for there to be a basic requirement; if you want to be an MP, then you must have either been born and raised in the area you want to represent or at the very least, lived and worked in that area for a minimum of five years. This is of course, something of a contradiction to the idea of being free to live and work where you choose, but it may also fall into the category of being one of those limits we freely accept. If that is, an MP is to be truly representative of the area they wish to serve.

On top of that, if the selection of an 'official' party candidate is left in the hands of a local committee, or imposed by the party itself, it may be time for independent party candidates to stand (and be funded through taxation). Thus a constituency will have a Labour Party candidate, an Independent Labour party candidate – or even more than one, as well as the same for other parties and those independent of any party. Primary elections would then allow constituency voters to ultimately select the final candidates to stand – and if an official party candidate was not voted through the primaries…tough.

There is still the question of MPs being out-of-touch, becoming unrepresentative of their constituents and having become MPs early in life, doing nothing else except being a career politician. This can be avoided very simply. Nobody becomes an MP before the age of, say, forty-five, thus giving them some twenty years of having to earn a living like everybody else. Secondly, their time in parliament is limited to no longer than twenty-five years. That takes them up to the age of seventy – which seems like a good time to retire.

One other thing that has been graphically demonstrated as being unacceptable to millions across the UK recently has been the inability to sack a bad MP. However, the Recall of MPs Act 2015 does make provision for constituents to be able to recall their MP and call a by-election. It received Royal Assent on 26 March 2015 after being introduced on 11 September 2014. There are some catches though; the Act does not allow constituents to initiate proceedings. Instead, a recall is initiated only if an MP is found guilty of a wrongdoing that fulfils certain criteria. These are:

> A custodial prison sentence of a year or less — longer sentences automatically disqualify MPs without need for a petition;
>
> Suspension from the House of least 10 sitting days or 14 calendar days, following a report by the Committee on Standards;
>
> A conviction for providing false or misleading expenses claims.

Thus far there has been three. The first was triggered against the DUP's Ian Paisley Jr when he received a 30-day suspension from the House of Commons. With just 9.4% of constituents signing, the recall was unsuccessful. The other two however, saw both MPs lose their seats. The first was Labour's Fiona Onasanya who received a prison sentence for lying over a speeding conviction. Her constituency of Peterborough was held by Labour although widespread allegations of vote-rigging and fraud over postal voting still surround the by-election that followed. The second saw the Conservatives' Chris Davies removed over false expenses. Remarkably, Davies was re-selected by his local association, who thus ignored voter's concerns. Unsurprisingly the by-election was won by the Liberal Democrats. If there was ever a fine example of the need for an Independent Conservative candidate, it was this one. Both by-elections were held in 2019.

So what about actually voting? The UK has a long-standing tradition of leaving the choice as to who one votes for and whether to vote at all to the individual. There has been some suggestion that voting should be made mandatory but if that were the case then the freedom of the individual is eroded even more than it is already. In any democracy worth the name, the ultimate freedom of choice is whether or not to cast a vote and then to which candidate that vote is given. However, if a majority of people choose not to vote, then a minority do so, which means that whichever political party gains power, it is not representing the majority. Under such circumstances, can any party forming a government truly say it has a mandate from the people to govern? Not really.

Now look at it a little differently - okay, so you don't vote. *'Politics? 'Not interested, not for me, they never listen anyway, so what's the point?'* If you don't vote, then you don't have the right to moan if you don't like what the Government does. Or what your local council does. So not only should you vote, you should actively seek out those elected (whether you voted for them or not), your MP, your local councillor, and ask them what they are doing for you and in your name, since you are one of those who gave them their job to start with and you are paying their salary (you are in charge, you pay your taxes – remember?).

Apart from that, if only a minority of people do vote, there is a chance – a good chance - that a rather oppressive movement gets its grimy paws on the levers of power; power over you.

Put another way, bad politicians get elected by people who don't vote.

■

4 Law and Order, Crime and Punishment

A hundred suspicions don't make a proof

Fyodor Dostoyevsky (Crime and Punishment)

Justice can only be reactive; it must never be proactive. Yet increasingly, justice has been dressed up as a reason to bring in more laws telling us what we cannot do and criminalising people who, however unintentionally, fall foul of those laws - and it is increasingly the case that people are arrested, charged and found guilty...before they have done anything.

Let me draw an analogy – a football referee's first job is to enforce the Laws of The Game. That much is fairly obvious and it is why the referee is there – if twenty-two people could play a game and play by the rules, the referee wouldn't be needed. But referees are criticised because, in the words of team managers, 'They don't protect gifted players.'

How does a referee 'protect' a player? What does the phrase actually mean? When managers use the term, they mean referees producing a red card and sending the clogging, fouling thug off...okay – let's look at that a little more; two teams turn up to play. The referee turns up. Player A on team B is known to dislike player C on team D. Everybody knows that player A is going to break player C's leg the first chance he gets. Player A has said he is going to. Player C knows his leg is going to be broken. The referee knows that player C is going to get his leg broken. If he plays...if he doesn't, then the thug, the bad guy – player A – wins and C becomes an oppressed, cowed and beaten individual. So he plays...he wants the freedom to decide for himself to play, to take the risk of the leg break (and not be told he is not allowed to play in case player A 'might' break his leg).

So what does the referee do? He *could* go up to player A before the game starts and say, 'Look, we all know what you are going to do, so I'm sending you off now to prevent you doing it.'

"But I haven't done anything,' replies player A. 'How can you punish me for something I haven't done?'

The referee can't.

So player A goes on to the pitch and takes part. Not long into the game, he does indeed break player C's leg and the referee then sends him off. Everybody nods and says, 'Yes, the referee was right to send him off for what he did...'

Player C however, still has the broken leg.

So how can the referee protect him? The referee can do NOTHING…until an offence has been committed. The same applies to the Criminal Justice System and those who work within it. Including the Police.

Ever heard of Strict Liability? Few have. There are two kinds of Law when it comes to breaking it. The most obvious is that which sees somebody charged with a more minor offence and thus appearing in a Magistrates Court, where a jury is not used – only the Magistrates decide on guilt or lack of it. The alternative is a Crown Court, in front of a Judge. Crown Courts are the ones we read about and see in a TV drama or on the news, the court in which a trial is held with a jury. The defending barrister, complete with billowing gown and wig, will (for the most part) effusively defend his client and the prosecuting barrister, with equally billowing gown and wig, will just as effusively try to persuade the jury that the defendant is as guilty as hell and needs to be locked up.

In law, all offences have what is termed 'a defence' – there is a list of allowable defences applicable to most offences so one cannot simply say what one likes to refute an allegation. The reason for this is simply to prevent spurious excuses being made to justify what might have been done and the same applies to offences; there is a list of what is and isn't an offence, which can, on occasion, lead to some confusion over what a suspect is charged with when something happens. It can also lead to unjust convictions.

For example: a factory owner is strapped for cash and decides to burn down his factory to get the insurance money. He does so at night because the working day is over and there is nobody in the place. Unknown to the owner however, somebody is working late and dies in the fire. The owner is then charged with murder. His defence would be that of being unaware of somebody present in the factory since it was closed for the day and nobody was supposed to be there. He would not therefore be guilty of murder (he might well be guilty of manslaughter and definitely of fraud but not of murder).

Put another way – the owner must intend for somebody to die. For him to be convicted of murder, two things must be present; the act itself (that of burning down the factory) and the intent (that of deliberately wanting to kill somebody). We know the act took place; the factory is a burned out shell. But the owner wanted to solve his financial problems; he never wanted or intended to kill someone.

The same principles apply to most offences; 1) proof must be shown that the act took place and 2) the result was what was intended. You must have the act *and* the intent. If either element is missing, a conviction cannot be made. With our footballer above, we know he had the intent, he said so himself - but what if he never actually carried out the act? He would not be guilty of anything.

Strict Liability however, is a different thing. With this, only the act is necessary. The most common use of strict liability is drunk driving; you have too much, get in your car and drive it. Use of a breathalyser shows that you were over the limit, you were in your car and you were driving – so you have no defence. You are guilty. You cannot say that you were at home having a drink and had no intention of driving anywhere but received a phone call to say your children had been in an accident and were in hospital. The quickest way to get to hospital was for you to drive, even though you aren't actually drunk (but still over the limit), you are in control of yourself and your car. You are still guilty. You have no defence.

Even though your children were indeed in an accident and really are in hospital – you have no defence, you are guilty. The accident to your children can be used as mitigation and you probably won't go to prison under such circumstances but you are still a drunk driver. You are guilty and you WILL have a criminal record.

Strict Liability does have some limits and, theoretically at least, cannot be imposed on a defendant if it does not apply. However, there are an increasing number of cases in which strict liability has been used to get a conviction and most especially in cases concerned with terrorism and child abuse. Both evoke an emotional response, with justification, and both are terrible things - but can one really justify misusing Strict Liability to get what then becomes an easy conviction?

Let me give you an example and one that will arouse that very emotional response from almost everybody; that of child pornography and via the internet. It is an awful thing and adults who deliberately involve themselves in it deserve condemnation. However…anybody who knows anything about computers will tell you that there are a number of ways in which something can be installed on your computer without you knowing it - the most obvious example is a virus of some kind. Many viruses are a nuisance rather than anything particularly harmful, but you don't know the virus is present until you turn your computer on and find it behaves differently to the way it did when you last used it.

In other words, the virus is put on your computer by somebody else and unknown to you.

A virus is often the product of the malicious and is nothing more than electronic vandalism; people create them because they can and despatch them around the world because they have the know-how to do so. In the same way, there are examples of people who know how to, sending a computer programme which places child pornography (or a link to it) on one's computer without the owner and user knowing that it is there. The porn is hidden. All computers have hidden files on them and these files are usually to do with making the computer work properly, which is why they are hidden – to prevent the unknowing (which is most pc users and this includes smartphones and any device capable of connecting to the internet) from accidentally deleting them. Files containing almost anything can thus be downloaded and remain hidden with the computer's owner or user completely unaware that they are there.

There has indeed been a recent and well publicised example of this very thing; Damien Green MP was effectively Prime Minister Theresa May's deputy and a holder of ministerial office before becoming so. In 2008, under the last Labour Government, that of Gordon Brown, the Home Secretary was Jacquie Smith, otherwise known as 'Jackboots Jacquie' for the number of oppressive laws that had been brought in under her stewardship of the Home Office. Green's House of Commons office *and* his home were raided by the Police, raids led by then Scotland Yard assistant commissioner Bob Quick. The raids were the result of a complaint by Smith that Green had leaked official figures regarding Labour's immigration policy and a memo which showed that an illegal immigrant was working as a cleaner in the Commons. Green's computers were taken away in the raids. No evidence was found and the case eventually dropped.

Yet in 2017, *nine years later*, now retired, Mr. Quick alleged that hard-core pornography had been found on Green's House of Commons computer. A similarly retired detective called Neil Lewis was the officer who examined the computer and he supported the allegations made by Quick. Although there was no question of the images being illegal, the furore that resulted ended in Green's resignation from the Government. He had maintained that he had not downloaded the images and knew nothing about them. As it subsequently transpired that he *did* know about them, he was obliged to resign, but – he continued to maintain that he did not download them himself. Support for this stance came from the Deputy Speaker of the House of Commons, Eleanor Laing MP.

In a letter to Mr Green, Mrs Laing says it was clearly possible at the time for pornography to find its way onto parliamentary computers without the knowledge of the user. In that letter, dated November 14, 2017, she stated:

> 'A member of my parliamentary staff has told me that, several years ago, before we had effective screening of our parliamentary computers, she used to find pornographic images on her computer every morning when she switched it on.
>
> 'She was certainly not accessing pornographic sites deliberately or even accidentally. The material was just there on her computer every day. She simply deleted it. This happened before 2010.

> 'Thus, it would appear that material found in the parliamentary computer system can be proved to have been put there by some other means than by the deliberate actions of the person operating the computer.'

This still applies today to the ordinary, everyday user of the home computer (or, again, any device that can connect to the internet).

The American FBI spends a great deal of time, effort and money in tracking child pornography, often passing on information to Police in other countries, including the UK. That information, acquired as a result of tracking illegal internet traffic and *even if incomplete*, has led to the dawn raid on a surprised recipient who has never done anything wrong and his computer seized and taken away; when it is forensically examined, what appears to be child pornography is found. The computer's owner, who freely says the computer is his, nobody else uses it or has access to it, is then charged with child porn offences...even though he has never looked for it, seen it or downloaded it.

The material however is present on his computer; the computer is his, nobody else uses it or has access to it. Because of this, Strict Liability is directly - or indirectly – imposed. The computer is ordered to be destroyed and the owner goes to prison and is labelled for life as a child sex offender - despite being completely innocent.

The mark of a free society? Hardly. Justice? Even less so. Yet there are, now, thousands of innocent people carrying such convictions. So why do it? Why is Strict Liability misused in this way?

Because it is easy. Because the emotions provoked by such a case means people simply want to follow the herd and point the finger. Getting convictions looks good on Police clear-up records and some pygmy career politician can preen in front of the media and say, 'Look how tough we are on crime'.

Author John R. Bradley, in an article for the Daily Mail wrote; '...Why should we not go one step further and electronically tag Islamist terror suspects so we always know where they are? They should also, like sex offenders, be banned from using the internet.'

In days gone by, when search and seizure resulted in suspect books or magazines being found, such items were correctly seized as evidence and used in court, as they are today. If a guilty verdict was reached, it would not however, have occurred to anybody to ban the person concerned from having all and any books or magazines.

Today, the internet is the modern equivalent. Even so, books and magazines still exist and are acquired by huge numbers of people (you're reading this for a start). Still today, at least to the best of my knowledge, there has never been a court-imposed ban on *all* books and magazines because somebody had a dodgy one. Yet, at least until recently, it has been extraordinarily common for the courts, encouraged by the Police, for an offender to have a ban placed on them from using and owning a computer and/or a mobile phone and accessing the internet. As John R. Bradley suggested, for those suspected of terrorism (not proven to be guilty, only suspected of it) there is a desire to have the internet entirely removed from such people, the same desire existing for sex offenders.

Bradley however, is wrong in two respects; firstly, one simply cannot impose a ban on computers, phones and use of the internet. Rightly or wrongly, all three are now a vital and integral part of ordinary life in today's society. Without them, nobody can live any kind of worthwhile life or pursue any lawful employment – there are very few jobs that, one way or another, do not need some kind of internet access and there are an increasing number of jobs that involve working from home using it. However, one *can* monitor the internet activities of somebody – provided they have been found guilty of illegal use and evidence of that presented in open court for all to see. Such monitoring is entirely justified and with modern technology, easily done.

But a complete ban on internet use is unjustifiable and is the mark only of the bully and the dictator. Not of a free society. Not of a society willing to take the risks associated with real freedom.

Bradley is also wrong in his remark concerning sex offenders being banned from the internet. They aren't, and for the reasons already stated, cannot be. Again however, a genuinely guilty sex offender can have their internet activities monitored and they are, quite extensively as it happens.

The everyday and all encompassing use of the internet has been cited as the reason for not imposing such bans and retrospective court action by offenders has resulted in changes to the Law; whereas at one time, these bans were imposed, today they are less likely but – and it is a big but – monitoring of internet activity has become the norm, *including* monitoring those who have not been charged with committing any offence or been found guilty of committing one.

You may or may not be an extensive user of the internet but consider how dramatic the adverse effect on your life if, for whatever reason and however innocent you may be, your name arose in some investigation and as a result, the Police came to your door at 7.30am, just as you were getting ready for or about to leave for work. Your job is on hold at least for that day and by the end of it, your ability to order something over the internet, your ability to contact your relatives and friends more or less instantly (regardless of where in the world they may be) has gone. You can no longer call somebody or send an email. Your property has been taken away - and if you need your computer and the internet for work, that's your job gone as well. Having removed your ability to communicate and travel (your phone will also be taken by the way, along with your passport in case you 'might' do a runner) the Police routinely seize so much property that it can take a year or more (yes, really, *a year or more*...as long as twelve months and counting) for them to get around to looking at it. Seized property is stored by the Police until they work their way through whatever other cases they may have and can get to you.

Meanwhile, unless you have the money to replace the seized equipment, that's you done for. Yet you haven't, at this point, even been charged with an offence - and if you haven't done anything wrong, you won't be (unless the Police lie, which has been known).

You think it can't happen to you? Yes it can.

It happens to people just like you and every day. You probably haven't done anything illegal and have never thought of doing so. Even if you haven't, you can still be investigated and even if not charged, particularly since it takes so long to deal with, your life has still been adversely affected - or even destroyed completely.

Did you know the Police do not need a search warrant to enter your home, search it and take away whatever they wish?

No? Didn't think so...well, they don't.

For the most part, if the Police want to raid somewhere, they do need a warrant, issued by a Magistrates Court, which empowers them to enter a home or workplace, search for and seize something specific. That something is usually directly related to the reasons given for requesting the search warrant. The police however, routinely abuse this by seizing anything and everything they can on the basis that anything and everything 'might' have evidence connecting it to the reasons for doing the search.

Oh, and by the way – requesting a search warrant means just that; asking for one. The police do not have the right to demand a search warrant and they must give sound reasons to the Magistrates for asking. Magistrates however, are not legal professionals. They are not lawyers. Magistrates are ordinary people who volunteer their time to sit as Magistrates so they don't usually refuse a police request for a search warrant (although it does happen). A Police request for a search warrant is also uncontested, meaning that there are only two parties involved; the magistrates and the Police. The subject, or target, of the warrant knows nothing about it until the Police come calling, usually at some early hour of the day. Granted, there would be little point in searching for anything if advance notice was given (thus allowing the target to attend a Magistrates hearing to say why the Police should not be given a warrant). Nevertheless, it remains the case that the system is heavily weighted in favour of the Police and thus the state.

One thing a search warrant does *not* mean is an arrest; as remarkable as it may seem, merely because they have been given the power to raid you and take away your property and possessions, it doesn't mean they have reason to arrest you. Put another way, the police want to investigate you and find out if there is, in fact, a reason *to* arrest you. So having searched and seized, but not arrested, the police may then invite you to the local nick to be interviewed, usually under caution, but since you have not been arrested, you are free to leave at any time - but your home has still been violated and your personal possessions rifled through and taken away.

So how come the Police can get away without a warrant? They can – and often do – simply arrest you as the starting point. To do so, all they need is 'reasonable suspicion' that you 'might' have committed an offence (or commissioned an offence to be made) and they can pick you up whenever and wherever they want - and it is the wherever that counts.

By using the Police and Criminal Evidence Act 1984 and its subsequent amendments and additions, all the Police need to do is arrest you and under the provisions of that act (also known as PACE) they can then search 'the place where the suspect last was' and take anything they wish. So if they turn up at your home at 0730am, arrest you on suspicion of doing something, since the last place you were when arrested was your home…they can search it and seize anything that they think 'might' constitute evidence of a crime or a crime being commissioned.

The term 'reasonable suspicion' is also one of the most wide-ranging definitions one could wish for. It can be, and often is, applied to so many ordinary (and law-abiding) activities, it makes your head spin, and it gives the Police enormous power. Keeping that in mind, the official guidelines for entering somebody's home and searching it state that, 'entry must be made at a reasonable time'. What is reasonable to one however, is not necessarily reasonable to another. The Police have been known to hammer loudly on a front door, or break it down at 0445am…or 0600am. Yes, really – quarter to five in the morning…and six in the morning. That is not reasonable by any definition - and it is not reasonable only because of the effect on the person being woken up at that time of day. It is also not reasonable because of the adverse effect on one's neighbours. In any residential street, banging on the door (or busting it in) at 0445am, is going to wake everybody up.

If you – or a neighbour – can be 'done' for playing music too loudly (along with a host of other things that cause problems for other residents), so can the Police. The Police do not make the law and they are not above the law. They are subject to it just like everybody else. Yet the British Police have fallen into the same, or similar, methods and bad habits, as one Court Judge succinctly put it, 'as those found in a banana republic' (the Judge concerned was actually referring to a case of postal vote fraud but the principle is the same).

The Police have two fundamental duties; the first is to investigate, fairly, without any bias and with an open mind, the possibility that wrong-doing may have been done.

The second is even more important; I would argue it is *the* most important duty the Police have - to investigate the possibility that wrong-doing has *not* been done. In that duty, they fail miserably. As they do when it comes to the fairly, without any bias and with an open mind part. That the Police need to investigate is not open to question; *how* they do so is.

The Police also cannot *prevent* crime; they can only pursue it.

When considering the possibility that a crime could be committed, there is a certain amount that the Police can do in advance of something happening, but they can only do so by pursuing evidence based on what somebody does or is doing – not what they haven't yet done or what they 'might' do. That means putting somebody under some kind of surveillance. Again it is one of those things we as ordinary people consent to; we give the state our permission for its agents – the Police or appropriate security service – to look at what we are doing, where we going and listen to what we are saying and to whom. The problem is that the greater the power given, the more likely it is to be abused. Human nature is what it is, so we must be extraordinarily careful with regard to how much power is granted and the way in which that power is used - and it remains a fact that the lines between the acceptable use of such power and what is oppressive and over-used have become more indistinct. The difference between what is genuinely necessary and what is merely desirable has been lost...the willingness to take the risks of freedom and of being free...

Let me illustrate the point; somebody walking through a park, a passer-by, sees a person of mature years hanging about with some young children and taking photographs of them. Even though, of itself and by itself, that isn't necessarily suspicious or even against the law (neither activity is). Such is the febrile nature of UK society today however, the passer-by then does what they think they are supposed to do and calls the police to report what they have been effectively brain-washed into thinking *is* suspicious.

The Police then send a group of officers steaming into the park (and sometimes a large group) to descend on the person of mature years and the children. They barrel up to the person and demand to know who they are and what they are doing to these children and why are they taking photographs of them.

It turns out that the mature person is the kids' Grandmother on an afternoon picnic and has taken the pictures for the family album. The scary part is that this has happened and has happened more times than most people are aware of.

It might help if a pair of officers were to amble casually by, and say, 'Hi, how are you this afternoon?' and engaged everybody in light conversation to find out what is actually going on, if anything. They might even get a cup of tea and a sandwich out of the occasion. But that isn't how it is done. It is done with force and in an intimidating manner - which yet again, is not the hallmark of a free society and one willing to take the risks of being free.

The sad aspect to the way in which the Police conduct themselves, and contrary to the example above, is that, for the most part police officers are good people. They will (and have done countless times, some very recently) put their lives on the line to protect others. Most are honest, hard-working and unstinting in their commitment to keeping everybody safe. No praise can be high enough for the dedication to duty shown by the majority.

But they are also hindered by the political correctness of those who are in charge of them and they are hindered even more by career politicians, who see the Police as simply a means by which their own desires to modify society can be imposed on ordinary people.

Ask yourself a question – most people will accept that for a society to work there must be rules, and most people will accept that human nature means there will be a minority who for one reason or another, will break those rules. Some may do so deliberately, some without knowing it and some completely inadvertently.

The question is this - when that happens, *as it will*, do you want justice…or do you want revenge? There is a difference.

The United Kingdom gave up killing its citizens many years ago, and with good reason. It was accepted that no matter how robust the system, no matter how excellent the checks and balances, the possibility exists that a mistake may be made and if the death penalty is applied, an innocent person *dies*.

That possibility still applies today. And it is *the* most important reason why capital punishment should remain outlawed. If that premise is accepted, it follows that the ultimate sanction is the deprivation of liberty – a spell in prison.

Prison is often a misunderstood concept to those who have never been in one, or who may not know anybody close to them who has. Many people who have not been anywhere near a prison often see newspaper headlines about a 'soft, easy life' for those doing time and are quick to suggest the regime should be harsh and unforgiving. Which then begs another question; do you send people to prison *for* punishment, or do you send people to prison *as* punishment? As with justice or revenge, there is a difference. One can tell a lot about a society by the way it treats those it chooses to lock up.

If one accepts the premise that one goes to prison *for* punishment, then you can be as harsh as you like. But if one also accepts that there are different kinds of offences, with some more serious than others, a prison where punishment is doled out will be just as harsh for the first-time minor offender as it will be for the career criminal on his or her umpteenth time inside.

On the other hand, if going to prison is the punishment itself – the loss of the thing that should matter most to the human spirit, freedom – then it follows that prison should not be a place where one is treated harshly but a place where one can learn from the mistakes that put you in it. Most importantly, a place where one can be taught how to live a law-abiding life.

Re-offending rates in the UK are absurdly high so clearly something isn't working.

The UK has got into the habit of using prison as a first resort. We lock more people up than any other in Europe and yet we still have a greater crime rate than other European countries. We 'warehouse' large numbers of people and do little to correct the behaviour that brought the prison sentence to start with. At the end of the time served, an offender is shovelled out the door with some £48 and left to it. Little or nothing is done to ensure that the now ex-offender has a life to go to. Or even a home…

As a society we need the commitment to be made to ensure that prison sentences are correctly applied and served, but also to ensure that people sent to prison leave it with something to offer themselves and society at large; that they can become ex-offenders in the truest sense and will not be discriminated against once they have paid their debt to society. This also means addressing the behavioural traits that are so often prevalent in society at large today, for example binge-drinking, a lack of respect towards other members of society, particularly the elderly and a multitude of other social attitudes that have not been tackled by successive governments. We need to address the bad attitudes that are the legacy of those who grew up in the 1950s, 1960s and 1970s

But we also need to address how the system works, before an offence is committed, after it, how it is dealt with and how a suitable punishment is put into effect. Prisons themselves need to be re-evaluated and redesigned; a modern prison, built today, looks remarkably similar, in terms of layout and operation, to those built in the 1800s.

▫

Clearly, there exists bad Law. Some Laws have been shown to be unnecessary or poorly thought out and have unintended consequences. Yet few are repealed. Why? Again, it serves the purpose of the state and its agents (including the Police) to keep bad law in place and a significant amount of law brought in to protect the public from terrorists or paedophiles falls into this category. So what can be done about it?

There are two ways to change the law; the first is in a Court of Law. Judges often say that they do not make the law and that laws are made in Parliament, which of course, is true. What Judges can do however, is challenge bad law by the judgements they make. Independent of politics, Judges can influence existing law and cause new laws to be made by their decisions and if presented with a case that has arisen because a law is a bad one, then the Judiciary can cause bad law to be changed.

The second way is to see your MP (the one you gave the job to) and demand that bad law is repealed.

The problem is…everybody has to do so. Are there enough people willing to do what is necessary and demand the changes that are needed?

Are you?

5 History and Hysteria

You can tell a lot about a society by what it fears.

Vejas Gabriel Liulevicius

News item – apparently a man has to tell the police at least twenty-four hours before he has sex…I promise you I'm not making this up. It seems he was accusing of raping a woman he knew but was cleared at trial. He is therefore not a criminal. Even so, the Judge described him as a 'very dangerous individual', so the police got what is now known as an Interim Sexual Risk Order, or SRO. Under the terms of the order, he is obliged to tell police the name, address and date of birth of any woman 'he intends to engage in sexual activity with' at least a day in advance. He is also banned from sending any text messages or making any calls unless fully operational offending and detection software is installed on his phone. This follows the change in the rules which give the police power to restrict the freedom of 'potential' sex offenders - even thought they have never been convicted of any offence. The same kind of thing is also being applied to 'possible' terrorists.

As I have already said, justice, if it is to be truly just, cannot and must not be proactive; it can only be reactive. In other words, somebody has to do something and then be called to account for it. You cannot and must not impose a punishment on people because they 'might' do something.

It is the risk of being free and the clue with the SRO is in the name; the Sexual Risk Order.

These orders have their roots in previous court orders which were found to be seriously flawed after their introduction by the Labour Government of Blair and Brown. The orders were headline-grabbing initiatives that looked good and demonstrated how Blair was living up to his claim of being 'Tough on crime. Tough on the causes of crime'. It was only after numerous legal challenges were successfully carried out that they were changed and morphed into the Sexual Risk Order of today.

The question however, remains; can we, as a free society, really eliminate entirely risk? Once again I make the same point – not if we are truly a free society.

□

We have a big hang-up in the UK about sex. So let's try and establish a few facts first.

Sex feels nice. It does. There is no getting away from it. Why does an act that can last a very short time or, when done with a little more experience and expertise, be an explosive and lengthy period of pure pleasure for the persons involved, feel so nice?

Because it encourages us to reproduce. In a nutshell, that's it – if we don't do it, we cease to exist. So the urge to reproduce is one of the strongest instincts we have as a species. Theoretically therefore, we could be banging away all day every day - but we aren't and we don't. We don't because there are sound reasons for us not to. Those reasons however, have little to do with the artificial restrictions placed on sex by society, restrictions that, for the most part, have their origins in religion.

Those artificial restrictions have resulted in something called 'sex-offending' (as opposed to any other kind of offending), and has done so because of the laws that prohibit doing certain things.

News report – Daily Mail Saturday March 18, 2017.
Headline –
'Student admits raping girl of 12…and walks free'.

"OMG! He got off with it!"
"What kind of lunatic is the judge for not jailing the perv for life?"
….Along with similar comments on social media, most put more earthily and using profanities by the bucketload, to describe the 'scum' who raped a child of twelve…but wait – you haven't read the article yet!
"Don't need to. That headline says it all…"
No it doesn't!

That's the problem, one of them anyway, with sensationalist newspaper headlines. They are designed to attract your attention and make you buy the paper before anything else, and given our love of being shocked, then you might read the article. If you read it properly, and the report is not slanted heavily in favour of making you angry, it might reveal a lot more.

In the case of the student who 'raped a twelve-year-old girl', he met her in a taxi queue after a night out and the two of them went on to an all-night party, during which, they paired off and had sex. In the morning the girl went home. Earlier in the evening, attending an unrelated incident, local police had no concern over the girl's apparent age and the taxi driver testified that he thought she was around twenty years of age. The student, then aged nineteen, thought she was seventeen or eighteen.

In other words, far from being a sweet little jelly-baby-munching-pigtail-wearing child, this girl was a big, buxom young lady who knew fine well what she was doing. The incident also raises one immediate question; no matter how busty she may have been, what was a twelve-year-old doing on a night out and then attending an all-night party somewhere?

Whatever the level of parental supervision (or lack of it) she was still twelve...so in law, the student had no defence. Only those aged thirteen and over are considered in law to be capable, mentally speaking, of giving consent, even though sex involving anybody under sixteen is illegal. That's why he was guilty of 'Statutory Rape'. Not of rape itself but an artificial definition of one person committing an act against another - hence the newspaper headline. The incident only came to light because days later, the girl thought she might have got pregnant, saw her GP, who told her to go to the Police and the girl's older sister then reported it. Not the girl herself - her sister.

The student admitted that the two did have sex and pleaded guilty since he had no legally allowable defence, and the circumstances meant that, like others, *including the Police*, he had been fooled by the girl's appearance.

The Judge took a pragmatic view and commented that the girl had been quite willing to have sex (a point that was never denied by the girl), looked much older, and had the incident occurred only a few months later the student *would* have had a defence – that of the girl's appearance – since she would have been thirteen by that time. So the student was given an absolute discharge.

Predictably there were howls of outrage from those worthies working in the child protection industry, along with the local MP, but an absolute discharge is not quite what the term seems to mean; it means simply that no further action is to be taken.

The defendant still has a criminal record as a sex offender however. So he didn't get off with it. That criminal record labelling him as a sex-offender will stay with him for the rest of his life even though he had no thought or intention of committing a crime, least of all a sexually motivated one (remember he was a teenager himself at the time, just – only nineteen but significantly therefore, an adult and thus charged and tried as an adult). Is this justice? Or revenge? And if it is revenge, for what?

A similar case arose when a middle-aged man met a younger man in an over-18s night club which also happened to be a gay club. The two began an affair which subsequently came to light and the younger man turned out to be fifteen.

So what was a fifteen-year-old boy doing looking for homosexual sex in an adult nightclub? The difference between this case and that of the twelve-year-old girl is that in law, a fifteen-year-old *is* considered to be mentally capable of consenting to sex, even though it is still illegal until sixteen. A twelve-year-old is not, no matter how physically well-developed they may be. So the middle-aged man was not guilty of rape, statutory or otherwise but, technically speaking and at least in law, he *was* possibly guilty of a child sex offence. Even though he was told by the younger person, that the younger person was eighteen. The older man had no desire, intent or wish to commit any offence and because he was deliberately misled by the fifteen-year-old, he had a defence and was found not guilty.

In both instances, Strict Liability was imposed and used to pursue the cases, even though neither offences are crimes of Strict Liability.

The big problem we have in the UK is our apparent willingness to believe the worst when it comes to sex and it has manifested itself alarmingly since the case of the late Jimmy Savile came to light. There has been a huge number of so-called historic sex offence allegations made, most of them against dead people and who thus cannot defend themselves, or those known to be rich (and famous). What makes these allegations interesting is that not too long before Savile, the Government published on its website details of the amounts of money available under the Criminal Compensations Scheme. This is the scheme that gives free and easy money out to anybody who has been the victim of a crime and significantly, no conviction is needed to get it. You just need to allege something and if convincing enough, its pay-day.

In Savile's case, there is little doubt that he, on the balance of probabilities, did indeed commit a number of offences. However…stop a moment. Consider the era in which most of those offences (not all but most) are alleged to have taken place; the 1960s and 1970s. This was a time in which sexual innuendo was rife; 'kiss-me-quick' and 'saucy' sea-side postcards; the Carry On movies, almost every one of which used sex as the basis for humour; a time when the old barriers came down, free love, anything goes, and did.

So how many of the allegations against Jimmy Savile were actually true? Let's take two examples – the first being that of a woman who alleged Savile raped her numerous times. She said (and I quote) '…he always used to wear his shell suits to do it so he could whip the trousers down quicker'. Savile was of course, well known for wearing a flamboyant shell suit and the woman alleged the incidents took place during the 1960s.

The shell suit was not invented until the late 1980s…

The shell suit's predecessor was the plain ordinary track suit worn by sports people and nobody in show business would be seen dead in a tracksuit; they were intended for use as training clothes for sports people. Not for pop stars and DJ's.

Now let's look at a second example – a relative of Savile claimed that at a family function, when she was still a young girl, he sat her on his lap and wriggled about beneath her. She said (and again I quote her) that she 'didn't know what the hard thing she could feel against her was.'

Her own family members, including the girl's mother, later said the occasion at which she alleged this to have happened never took place…and that's before we consider that paedophiles do not carry out their acts in full view of others; they commit their offences when nobody is looking, behind closed doors and unobserved.

Some of the allegations against Savile became more and more outlandish as time went on, apparently including the involvement of cadavers in hospital morgues. Was Jimmy Savile guilty of everything said of him? Nobody can really know. He's dead. So were the cadavers. They can't testify and neither can he. The significant aspect to this are the number of similar allegations made since Savile against others who are also dead. They cannot defend themselves so the test of a court trial can never happen. Yet we seem to be falling over ourselves to believe any allegation made against anybody. Why?

Why is it that the United Kingdom seems to have a child sex crisis, whereas other countries do not?

Is it because the industry that has sprouted around child protection now has an enormous number of people earning nice salaries out of it? To justify those salaries (and the media attention they get) they must have victims. The more victims they have the more power and influence they have. This is why the myth is propagated that the UK is filled with bad people all of whom have evil designs on our children - it is not.

More interestingly, there have been a number of cases where it has been subsequently shown that allegations against somebody are merely that; allegations and ones that have been proved to be untrue. The most infamous of these was the case of 'Nick', a fake name used to hide the identity of one Carl Beech, who made up stories against a number of very high-profile people and did so to get the compensation available There have been others, less well publicised but the aim was the same – easy money.

The UK has no more (or less) of a problem than anywhere else. We have simply sleepwalked into a trap of unthinkingly believing what the state tells us, to the point now where too many people, parents especially, think there is a paedo around every corner. No there isn't. People genuinely believe that it is against the law to take photographs of children. No it is not.

Yes, there are bad people out there and yes, we need to be aware and yes, we have a duty to teach our children of the possible dangers, both online and offline. What we should not be however, is frightened - and we must not teach fear.

Fear of the paedophile and fear of the terrorist must never be allowed to rule.

．

6 The EU, Immigration, Brexit and the Age of Legal Majority

*The European Union, which is not directly responsible to voters,
provides an irresistible opportunity for European elites to seize power
in order to impose their own vision on a newly socially regimented
Europe.*

Maggie Gallagher

*Author's note – some of this was written before the EU Referendum and
needs to be read in that context. It is updated later in the book.*

Please note the date of my first writing this – it was January 1, 2014. I
did so for a possible policy document for a political party. Which one
doesn't really matter but I note the date because there is one
important element of the European Union that has never, to the best
of my knowledge, been commented on or explained by anyone in
politics or mainstream media, at any point over the past sixty or
more years, although it has been briefly touched upon by German
Chancellor Angela Merkel and more recently by political
commentator Peter Oborne; it is why the EU exists in the first place.

The EU exists for one reason and one reason only; to stop
Germany, France, Belgium, The Netherlands, Luxembourg and Italy
from being torn apart by armed conflict again. Those six countries
were the founders of the EU, and more than any others, have been at
the centre of continent-wide war twice in modern history and
numerous times before 1914. And it is those six countries that have,
one way or another, suffered the most from those conflicts. By
binding those six together as closely as possible, politically,
economically and in every way that can be thought of, the European
project is to ensure that it is simply not possible for war to break out
between them again. If other countries can be drawn into this, and be
bound just as tightly to it, the chances of war are lessened still
further.

If one can grasp this and truly understand it, it becomes easier to
understand why the EU behaves as it does; why 'harmonisation' is
considered so important; why the single currency exists and why
free movement of people and trade is such a fundamentally
important part of the EU ethos and culture. Only by properly
understanding its reason for being to begin with can one make a
decision on whether or not to remain a member of it.

There is a strong case to be made for being in membership of the EU but there is also an equally strong case to be made for leaving it. If one is going to be in it, then it is logical to embrace the methods of running it and to equally embrace the positives *and* negatives of membership. One cannot sit on the fence and pick and choose which bits one likes and which bits one doesn't. What one *can* do is be the driving force behind the change that the EU undoubtedly needs - if one is a member of it.

If one is going to leave, the consequences of doing so need to be fully understood. Are there going to be any barriers to trade and industry? What barriers will be placed in the way of free movement of goods and people? Will any barriers at all be placed by the UK Government? Will any barriers be put in place by the EU itself? Are there any legal implications of withdrawal? Or legally binding obligations that would arise from withdrawal? Only by fully understanding ALL the ins and outs of being in or out can a decision be made.

Allied to the question of the EU is concern over the level of immigration into the UK. Even many within the Labour party, responsible for the biggest wave of immigration into the UK in history, now seem to accept that levels of immigration were too high during their time in office between 1997 and 2010.

Whatever the rights and wrongs, there is one reason and one reason **only** why immigration needs to be severely restricted, and perhaps even halted completely; geographically the UK is a small country. In terms of land area it is not the smallest, far from it in fact, but – *there is no more room*. The UK is at the limit of how many people can have housing; can be transported to and from work; be educated while of school age; be helped if ill.

 Nobody should be denied the right to come and live and work in the UK based on skin colour, religion, sexual orientation or for any other reason. The only determining factor is whether or not a person may come and live in the UK is that they have a job to come to.

It also needs to be borne in mind that there is a large number of UK citizens living and working in other countries, within both the EU and elsewhere.

2015 - Budapest in Hungary came to a complete halt because the main train station had been overrun with illegal migrants. The Hungarian authorities are applying the rules rigidly and saying the migrants will not be allowed to travel on until they have been through the registration process. The migrants are revolting and demonstrating and getting all upset that they can't just walk into any EU country they like, when they like, how they like.

A pair of very young Syrian children drowned in the Mediterranean

Sea. All the newspapers carried front page headlines about it. I have some sympathy with the innocent people of Syria and Afghanistan. Any death is tragic - but...predictably all the politicians were wringing their collective hands and saying we must take all these people in.

Why?

None are EU citizens. None have automatic right of entry to any EU country. Yet they all seem to think (including those who continue to break the law trying to bust into Britain from France) that they can just breeze their way into somebody else's house and make themselves at home. I don't care how desperate somebody is. If you want to get out of the hellhole you were unfortunate enough to be born in and go live somewhere else, then fine. There is a procedure to follow. So follow it.

The father of those two little boys who died apparently paid a people smuggler 5,000 Euros to travel illegally into a European country. 5,000 Euros....what's that in UK pounds sterling? Work it out...How many people in the UK, born and bred here, from Parents who were born and bred here, from Grandparents and Great-Grandparents born and bred here, have such an amount of money to spend on travelling somewhere?

Europe is only so big and no European country can afford to house and look after so many migrants.

The answer is twofold;

Hunt down and *stop* the smugglers, *permanently*, regardless of borders. Set up a number of secure reception centres, as many and as big as are needed, funded by *all* European countries (not just those in the EU) and take the migrants to them, whether they like it or not. At these centres they will be fed, clothed and given a roof over their head. They can be given any medical treatment they need. They can even be taught to speak different languages and be given training and education to get jobs - and they can be processed and sent on to the right country for them.

The right country might not necessarily be in the EU. There are other places in the world that are safe to go and live in.

Once the smugglers have been eliminated and people know full well that if they turn up at our borders they *will* go to a reception centre and simply will not be allowed to waltz into any EU country they want, they will stop coming in such huge numbers.

The place to start is on the borders of the country that they are fleeing from and in the next country to them; I see little sign of those countries lifting a finger to help their neighbours.

Rather remarkably, since I first wrote my comments about reception centres, this very suggestion has come to the fore, with the EU declaring that such centres are the answer. Predictably however, it has met with some considerable disquiet, not because of the validity of the idea itself, but how these centres will be paid for and where they will be located. Some countries in membership of the EU are against the idea if the centres will be only on their territory and they will be the ones who have to fund them. Understandably perhaps, countries like Spain and Italy are not keen but this also applies to Greece, which has had a serious problem with the numbers arriving there.

The Island of Lesbos, despite the name having some historic connotations, is also one of Greece's idyllic holiday hotspots, home to all the things one might expect of such a place. It is also however, the location of Moria, a former army barracks now use to house illegal migrants. Designed to house 3,000, it is now crammed with 7,356 people, most from Africa, but also many from Iraq, Syria and, perhaps more curiously, Pakistan. The camp is a squalid, inhumane cesspit of people trapped by EU inertia. Moria has become a symbol of EU countries bickering over who should do what and pay for it. Yet the solution is as I have already said; such centres need to be across European countries, to alleviate the strain placed on the initial point of arrival, must be funded by *all* European countries (including the UK) and not only by those in membership of the EU. On top of this, the ultimate destination for these migrants may not necessarily be a European country. Like I said, there are other countries around the world that are safe to build a new life in.

As well as being hospitable places of welcome, education and real help, the deterrent effect for those simply 'trying it on' (and such people aren't limited to one country or another) must be strong enough to stop those who don't need Europe's assistance.

Which includes those from Pakistan. Why are there people from Pakistan trying to enter Europe illegally? There are well-established Pakistani communities around the world, not least in the UK and there are equally well-established methods of moving from Pakistan to live in any of these countries.

One of the tasks of reception centres will be to weed out those who should not be there to start with, regardless of their country of origin and such people must be returned to where they came from, without fear or favour.

In mid-2016, the UK, by a not-too-great-majority, voted to leave the EU. What do people actually mean when, according to some newspapers at least, 'immigration' was the main reason for Brexit?

Lets look at some facts and I will say what nobody else has had the courage to say; if you walk down any street in any town that has a high number of immigrants from the EU, take a look at the faces. Don't listen to people talk – just look at the faces.

What you will see are white, Christian, European faces. Not black or brown African and Asian faces; just white and Christian. The only way to tell which EU country those immigrants are from will be to listen to people speaking Polish, German, French, Spanish, Italian or whatever language is spoken in those white, Christian, European countries.

By 'Immigration', what is *really* meant is immigration by non-Christian, black or brown people. Personally I rather like the idea of living in a country that has a wide mix of people from around the world and I don't care what their skin colour is and I don't care what their faith is.

By itself, immigration from EU countries is not a problem, has never been a problem and never will be a problem; numbers however, may be a different matter.

On Wednesday 29 March, 2017, Prime Minister Theresa May triggered article 50 and formally informed the EU that the UK would leave. The mayhem thus began…

Various EU noteworthies have spoken of 'punishing' Britain for daring to be independent, others have been conciliatory, but the two-year period of negotiation is apparently fraught with difficulty and will be a tortuous path, in which the UK will suffer or both the UK and the EU will suffer and so and so on *ad nauseum*.

Every news report, both print and broadcast, along with every politician in the UK and the EU has emphasised how 'difficult' it all is, with some suggesting that it will take a lot longer than the two-year period allowed for under article 50.

So let me make it very simple…

> The UK will remain a committed ally and friend of the EU and its member countries and will work as a dedicated and equal partner alongside and with the EU in all and every matter, including security, terrorism and crime.
>
> EU Citizens are entirely free to apply for employment in the UK, and once accepted for that employment, are welcome to come and live and work in the UK. EU Citizens are equally welcome to come and live in the UK if they are of independent financial means (meaning retired or just plain rich enough). All EU citizens are further welcome to visit the UK at any time for business, holiday or recreational purposes at any time and without restrictions or visas.
>
> No restrictions will be placed on the free movement of EU citizens to the UK for those reasons.
>
> The same will apply to UK citizens wishing to live, work and visit EU countries.

No restrictions, barriers or tariffs on trade or business movement will be placed by the UK on any Country in membership of the EU.

The UK will make its own trade arrangements with countries not in the EU.

There. What's difficult about that?

Undoubtedly there are those (and many of them) who will say, '*Ah yes, but what about....*' and come up with dozens of reasons why this or that can't be done, or why that or this is more complex.

That's easy. To say why something cannot be done takes no talent or vision. Taking the opposite view and saying why something *can* be done may be harder - but it can be done. Just stop making things complicated for no good reason other than being pissed off that somebody wants to be free, independent, make their own laws and control their own borders.

That is the EU's big mistake; to dominate and demand; to order and not suggest. On the other hand, by committing to a free trade and movement principle (that's free movement to work, *not* to sponge off welfare), it is still possible to do as the founders of the EU wanted, to bind free, independent countries together, to ally them closely, to make things work better.

And to avoid war.

□

There is another curiosity to the question of immigration and the right or otherwise of people to come to the UK (or for that matter, any country).

As mentioned, one of the tenets of the EU is the free movement of goods and people, which put simply, means that any citizen of any EU country can move between those countries, to live and/or work without restriction, as can businesses. This however, is *not* the same as saying those who wish to do so can do it without the means of identifying themselves. As it happens, some form of ID document is mandatory in most EU countries and people carry ID cards as a matter of course. Except in the UK...

To make movement easier, the Schengen Agreement came into being. This agreement allows anybody in any EU country to move between each without any means of identification at all – there are no borders between Schengen Agreement countries. Provided of course, a country has actually signed up to it – and the UK never has.

So, to travel between London and Berlin, a UK citizen needs a passport. To travel from Paris to Manchester, a French citizen needs a passport. The same applies between every EU country and the UK – you still have to have a passport (there is one exception to this but we will get to that momentarily). Put another way – if you haven't got a passport...you don't go. So the UK already has control of its borders. At least up to a point.

You don't need a Visa to go with your passport but a Visa is simply an endorsement of your passport from the country you wish to visit saying that your passport is in order, identifies you, is up-to-date and hasn't expired and there is nothing wrong with it (or with you).

So what is all the fuss about?

The fuss is that, as a member of the EU, technically speaking, the UK does not have the right to deny entry to an EU-passport holder. It does however, have the right to deny entry to anybody who does not have one...including all those illegal migrants in France.

There are two other oddities at work here; the first is that exception mentioned above; open borders have existed between the Republic of Ireland and the UK since the 1920s – you don't need a passport to fly between London and Dublin. Book a flight ticket with Aer Lingus on the Irish airline's busiest route and the carrier will tell you that a bus pass is a good enough means of identification to fly from Heathrow (although whether or not you will get a quizzing from an Irish Immigration Officer at the other end is another matter).

The UK and Ireland even have reciprocal voting rights.

That same principle applies to the border between Northern Ireland – a part of the UK – and the Republic of Ireland, the southern part, which of course, is a member of the EU.

Since there are no borders between the UK and the Republic of Ireland so people and goods can move as they please, then simple logic will tell you that after the UK leaves the EU, there should be no issues regarding passing from one to the other – there hasn't been for nine decades. The only problem arose in the 1970s and 1980s because of the terrorism threat from the IRA. The progress made in reducing that threat over recent times is not an excuse for saying there should, or will, be a problem around customs checks and so on. That hasn't existed between the UK and the Republic of Ireland for longer than most people today have been alive and the UK is the Republic's biggest single trading partner.

The port of Felixstowe (on the Sussex coast) can, and does, move a huge amount of cargo through it and into the UK swiftly and with little or no delays, both from the EU *and* from the rest of the world. Since the amount of similar business that will pass between the UK and the Republic of Ireland is tiny by comparison, a little imagination will solve any possible problems with equal swiftness. Unless of course, somebody wants to be deliberately obstructive to a deal between the UK and the EU.

The second peculiarity is that there are three countries that are not members of the EU – but *are* members of the Schengen Agreement; Switzerland, Iceland and Norway.

Yet the procedure for the UK to leave the EU is 'difficult'? Only if those responsible make it so.

Since I made my first remarks on the EU in January 2014, some of the points I raise above have indeed been made by others (remember who said it and wrote it first…two-and-a-half years *before* the EU referendum was called in the UK) although the ideal of preventing war hasn't been among them specifically.

A significant number of the most vocal opponents of Brexit are often heard to speak very disparagingly of those who voted to leave, tending to put leavers into one of two categories; leavers are racist or simply didn't know what they were voting for. Both descriptions are extraordinarily insulting and do no credit to those making them.

As time has moved inexorably on and the negotiations moved along with it, a number of things have become very apparent. One is that, if allowed to get away with it, the EU's position is that the UK will indeed be punished for daring to wish to be free. Yet it is only those employed by the EU itself that seem to wish to pursue this course. One by one, a number of EU countries' leaders are beginning to say that agreements and trade deals must be made – it is after all, in their interests. However, until and unless those leaders simply instruct the negotiators to stop blustering and get on with it, those with a vested interest in maintaining the status quo will try to prevail and it is those with their snouts deepest into the trough of EU funding that work the hardest at frustrating Brexit.

This is also being aided and abetted by those in the UK who want the country to remain. The problem however, is very simple (as are the solutions).

Democracy works in a very easy to understand way; everybody of age to do so is given the right to vote; that vote then decides something. Usually it is who the majority of voters want to run their country (or local authority) for them and on their behalf. Since everybody is not going to vote the same way, the majority wins. The minority, however significant, gives way, shuts up and campaigns for a different decision the next time round (in the UK, five years later). A referendum however, is a slightly different thing.

A referendum is when Parliament decides that something is too important to be left to it alone – only the will of those who elected them in the first place can decide on whatever it is that a referendum is held over. Put another way, it is for a majority of the people to decide and having made their decision, the Government, along with ALL other members of Parliament, must then carry out the decision.

A referendum is not 'advisory'. It is not a point of view open to discussion or negotiation. It is not to be ignored or dismissed. It is an instruction from the people to those who have been given their job by those people. Any other way of looking at it means a referendum is rather pointless and there is only one referendum. There is not a series of them, or another in five years so that the decision of the people can be changed next time round. In the case of remaining in or leaving the EU, the question was very simple; stay in or leave?

The UK was almost evenly divided over the answer but only almost; a majority view was that the UK must leave. Those who wanted the country to stay were in a minority. So of those, any that have, or are, trying to frustrate or change the result are betraying their country and democracy itself.

People like Dominic Grieve, Ken Clarke, Anna Soubry, Nicky Morgan, Antoinette Sandbach, Stephen Hammond, Heidi Allen, David Lammy and others, Conservative, Labour, Liberal Democrats, SNP or whatever, cannot stay in their positions as MPs if they feel that Brexit must be denied – they gave up the privilege of deciding that when Parliament handed the decision to the people. They must abide by it or resign as the people's representatives. If they will not step down voluntarily, they must be deselected by their constituencies (interestingly enough, as 2018 became 2019, there has been talk of this happening – see later).

The same applies to the UK parliament's second chamber, the House of Lords. The Lords do not and never have, decided how the UK is, or should be governed. That is the sole task of the House of Commons, the House of those the ordinary citizen gives their job to by electing them. The task of the Lords is to have another look at any law the Commons wants to enact and see if there is anything wrong with it. If it thinks there is, then it asks the Commons to think again. What the Lords cannot do is deliberately block or stop the Commons from doing what the people have told it to do.

Yet today, the principles of the House of Lords has become corrupted by deliberately stuffing it full of failed career politicians, political has-beens, those who are not has-beens because they have never been anywhere, sometimes crooked cronies and dodgy donors of money to political parties. It is a chamber crammed with those who have been appointed to it by the leaders of those same political parties, most significantly Tony Blair, Gordon Brown, David Cameron and Nick Clegg. All four did so to influence the Lords and how it operates.

The direct consequence now is that the House of Lords sees itself as the Guardian to the Gates of Britain. It, and significant numbers of its members, are an outdated, overblown anachronism that needs to be abolished. It is even, now, today, the world's second largest second chamber after China. If there was ever a reason for doing away with it, it is that one.

Also involved in all of this are 'the young'. By 'young' I mean those aged between sixteen and around twenty-five to thirty. Politicians are very fond of using the term 'young people' these days, which does beg an immediate question; if 'young people' are so important, what happens to them when they are no longer 'young'? Are they then of no importance? Nobody over thirty matters?

Logan's Run is coming...

Whenever a politician talks about employment, housing or a number of other things, I guarantee that those two words will be used; 'young' and 'people'. One of the elements to the political obsession with 'young people' is that the voting age needs to be lowered to sixteen. During the referendum campaign a number of sixteen and seventeen-year-olds were interviewed, all of whom stated they wanted to remain in the EU...why did nobody interview a sixteen or seventeen-year-old who wanted to leave? There are plenty of them. The most oft-stated comment from those who were interviewed was 'This is my future.' Well, so it is - but it is also the future of everybody else, including those who are no longer 'young' and those who are not yet sixteen. Or seventeen either. So if we give the vote to sixteen-year-olds, should we not also give it to fifteen-year-olds? Ten-year-olds? Heck, why stop there? Let EVERYBODY vote; the newly-born can be carried into the polling booth and can make their mark like everybody else – it is their future too.

Much is made of those who voted in the original referendum, over forty years ago, all of whom voted for entry into a free trade area, not the union of a large number of countries into one. I didn't get to have that vote however – I was far too young. So, according to today's mantra, my future was denied. No it wasn't. I was not yet of adult age. I had to wait. So must those who are not of adult age now. The answer to the voting age question is simple; there has to be a cut-off point somewhere, a point at which those things that are the preserve of adulthood remain so. You get to do them when you become an adult.

If one believes that the right age is sixteen, then fine. Let it be sixteen. But sixteen then becomes the age at which you can do all those things that adults do as well as vote. You can drink, drive, smoke, have sex, join the Army and get killed for your country. On the other hand, if one believes that sixteen is too young, then let it be eighteen. Once you reach that age, the age of legal majority, whatever age it is, if you think something that was done before you were old enough to have a say is wrong, then you have the right to campaign to change it.

But you have to get to that age first. Once you have, you are an adult. With all the rights - and the responsibilities - that come with it.

•

7 Human Rights

*Peace can only last where human rights are respected, where the
people are fed, and where individuals and nations are free.*

14th Dalai Lama

The Human Rights Act is often referred to by the Daily Mail
newspaper as '...the hated Human Rights Act...', or sometimes as
'...Labour's Human Rights Act...' Both descriptions are at best,
misleading and at worst untrue.

Hated by whom? And although it is true that the Labour
government of 1997-2010 incorporated the European Convention on
Human Rights (to give it its correct title) into British Law, thus
making it obligatory from the legal standpoint to follow its strictures,
it is often a misreported set of rules, all of which simply set out a way
in which a state should behave towards its citizens.

As with most other things it is important to understand both the
act itself and its reasons for being; its history and why it was thought
of to begin with. One of the aspects never reported is that the
European Act is based on the United Nations Universal Declaration
on Human Rights, signed by most countries in membership of the
United Nations in 1948 (although not all). The European Act follows,
word for word, the statements contained in the Universal
Declaration. The UK was one of the countries responsible for its
original drafting and is a signatory to both the Universal Declaration
and the European Convention.

Membership of the EU does not affect a country's moral obligations
to follow the two acts once they are a signatory to them; the
European Act is *not* a creation of the EU (neither is the European
Court) and membership or otherwise of the EU does not affect a
country's moral obligation to maintain the strictures of both Acts – if
they have signed them.

Neither act however, is inviolate law; unless a country chooses to
make them or one of them so, as Labour did after taking office in
1997. There is, put more simply, a moral obligation to follow them
once becoming a signatory to them. I would say that having
voluntarily chosen to sign both, the moral obligation is higher and
more pressing than a legal one.

The Universal Declaration is the most simple of the two. It was
created after WWII in an effort to place that moral obligation on
those countries signing it to behave in a certain way and to avoid

the situations and circumstances that, for example, led to the persecution of members of the Jewish Faith in Germany prior to and during WW2. It accords everybody a set of rights to which they should, as human beings, be entitled to. It contains no qualifications or catches. There are no exceptions to any of the rights contained within it.

The European Convention on the other hand, takes these matters several steps further. Whilst recognizing all the rights of the Universal Declaration, it also added a number of qualifications – the small print if you like.

It is these qualifications that are often misunderstood, misinterpreted or sometimes ignored altogether, particularly by British Courts of Law and most especially since the European Act was brought into British Law. These qualifications give Governments and their agencies power to override some of those rights if necessary, for example for law and order.

Take the right to privacy. There are no qualifications contained in the right to privacy within the Universal Declaration. The individual has an absolute right to privacy, in their home and correspondence (including emails and other electronic communications) to name just two. The European Convention on the other hand, whilst giving one the same right to privacy, allows the Police to enter your home and examine your correspondence if there is a justifiable reason for them to do so *and the country's laws permit it.*

A reminder – see earlier – that one of the aspects to police powers that is virtually unknown is that the Police in the UK do *not* have to have a warrant to search your home and take away your property…all they need to do is arrest you at your home and under the provisions of the Police and Criminal Evidence Act 1984, they may then 'search the place where the suspect last was' and seize anything that they believe 'might' constitute evidence of a crime or the commissioning of a crime. To arrest a person, all the police need is 'reasonable suspicion', probably one of the most wide-ranging and yet ill-defined clauses one could wish to find - but one that does not breach the European Convention on Human Rights…

Put another way, to get round the provisions of both the Universal Declaration and the European Convention, all a government has to do is pass a law that allows them to do so.

The Blair/Brown led Labour government was notorious for doing just this; over 3,500 new laws were passed between 1997 and 2010, often using the threat of terrorism or child protection to restrict and remove rights from the UK citizen. The commons majority held by New Labour throughout its time in office meant that opposition to these laws was often outvoted in the Commons by a comfortable margin.

Few have been repealed by the present government.

Derogation.
As said above, all a Government needs to do is pass a new law that allows it to disregard any part of the European Convention on Human Rights – and it can also choose to derogate from parts of the Convention.

What this means is that, to prevent terrorism for example, our Government can simply ignore the right we have to privacy and spy on us as much as it wants. It can arrest us and imprison us without charge or trial.

You will undoubtedly have encountered the term 'remanded in custody'. Do you know what it means? Some people will, many do not. It means that merely because you are suspected of doing something, you can be arrested and sent to prison for an indeterminate period of time *without being charged with an offence, without a trail taking place and without being found guilty of an offence.*

And it happens in the UK every day.

In 2009, I interviewed a number of remand prisoners; one was an Asian man who had spent over a year in prison on remand; he had not been charged with anything, he had not tried and been found guilty of anything - but he was still in prison. At this point it has to be conceded that there are certain persons and circumstances where taking somebody into custody without charges and a trial could be warranted, and the reasons for doing so are primarily to allow an investigation to take place and to prevent the suspect from doing a runner and disappearing. The other often-used possibility is that the suspect 'might' commit more crimes. Once a trial is held, time spent in prison already is then deducted from the sentence, so a two-year sentence becomes one year since the person concerned has already spent a year inside.

But what if they are found not guilty? What if the evidence doesn't stack up? What if it can be conclusively shown in court that the defendant did not commit the crime and had no intention of committing any crime? They have still spent time in prison and if that time is lengthy (and it often is) then their life has been destroyed; they come out with no job, sometimes no home and there is no compensation. There have even been cases of people remanded in prison, who have ultimately been found not guilty, released and then receiving a bill from HM Prison Service for the money spent on them while in prison (I'm not making that up – really, it has happened).

Yet this does not breach the Human Rights Act and no derogation is needed either.

So why is there a desire on the part of the Conservative Party to withdraw from the Human Rights Act?

Because it makes good headlines in some newspapers. Under David Cameron, the Conservatives made much of withdrawing from the European Act, repealing the law that Labour brought in to make it British Law, and creating what was termed a 'British Bill Of Rights'. What could such a bill say that would be different from the European Act? Or the Universal Declaration? The answer is, that if it were to mean anything, not a thing.

Such a Bill of Rights would be so watered down it would be utterly impotent.

If you don't know what the European Convention actually says, it is available, in full, on the internet. So is the United Nations Universal Declaration. Go look them up. Print a copy of both – don't leave it on your computer, print hard copies and keep them. Read both and read them carefully – neither are difficult to understand and both are couched in easily understood wording. Once you have read them – and most importantly the catches, that small print in the European version - you may well scratch your head and wonder why so many cases have arisen where the Act has been misused to stop the deportation of proven terrorists.

It is not the Human Rights Act that is the problem. How it is misused is.

Of all the countries around the world there is one that has stood like a beacon to the rest when it comes to the freedom of the individual and that is the United Kingdom. That standing is being steadily and remorselessly undermined and has been for at least the past twenty years, significantly and specifically since 1997.

Our Government – the one we elect - must clearly state a commitment to both the Universal Declaration and the European Convention on Human Rights (along with the European Court) and to commit to repealing many of the laws passed in recent times that do restrict the freedom of the individual. Our Government must lead the change that is needed to the European Convention to stop the misuse and abuse that happens now.

But as ever, it comes down to the individual citizen to demand that it does.

And that means you.

8 Our Caring Society

Normal is getting dressed in clothes that you buy for work and driving through traffic in a car that you are still paying for in order to get to the job you need to pay for the clothes, the car, and the house you leave vacant all day so you can afford to live in it.

Ellen Goodman

'I run a company. Ten years ago, I employed 200 people to run my business. Today, thanks to technological advances, I need only 100 people'.

That's 100 people who do not now have a job. Multiply that concept nationwide, add in an increased population and one thing becomes clear – the days when everybody could have a job of some kind are over. They were a number of years ago.

One of the great unspoken truths of modern day society is that it is not possible for everybody to be in work. It is time politicians spoke truthfully about this. The country therefore needs to accept that there will be a number of people who will need state help to survive and this number will inevitably be greater than in previous times and greater than most would like. However, this does not mean that people should be left to spend their days idly watching TV. There are a multitude of tasks that those in receipt of Job-Seeker's Allowance (JSA), Universal Credit or whatever names the Government gives to welfare, can do and should be doing in return for their benefits.

What one should *not* be doing however, is using the threat of cuts to benefits to ensure people *are* doing something useful. Neither should there be artificial conditions like 'applying for a minimum number of jobs per week' to keep the JSA payment at its usual rate. This number of jobs simply do not exist any longer.

It is interesting to note that the present and previous governments closed many job centres, or reduced the service and made people go online to seek employment *(see the above remark about technological advances and the earlier comments about banning people from internet access)*. What does one do if one does not have home internet access?

Computers cost money; paying the bill for home internet access costs money. Those people unable to afford them (and there are more than one might think) have to use their local library – if the local council has not closed it due to cuts…

Present government policies, whilst they may have good reason, are being used in a way that is at best not helpful, at worst entirely destructive in delivery.

Radical and new ways in which to deal with unemployment need to be found, including an acceptance that there will always be a higher unemployment figure than one would like to see and telling the truth about it (and not merely spouting interminably on about 'getting people back to work' when no government is truly able to give such a guarantee), and this must include removing the stigma from being out of work. It must also accept that many older people, whilst still below retirement age, may not be able to find work as many employers take the not unreasonable view that they would rather employ a thirty-five-year old on the basis that they will get some thirty or more years from that employee, and not somebody who will only be with them for a few years before retiring. This may come across as being somewhat ageist but in the interests of company stability, it is understandable.

One of the more iniquitous aspects to the Department of Work and Pensions, or DWP (and also under its previous names like the DHSS, which stood 'Department of Health and Social Security', but better known as the Department of Stealth and Total Obscurity), is that it has always seen its primary purpose as being that of preventing people from receiving benefits. It is notorious for the speed with which it stops benefits being paid and equally so for the slowness at which it starts paying them.

In times past, benefits were sent out every two weeks in the form of a Giro Cheque which could be cashed at a post office or paid into a bank account if the recipient had one. Today, all payments are made direct into a bank account. When benefits are stopped, often the first the recipient knows about it is when they go into their bank and find they have no money. A letter may then arrive either later that day or even days later, telling the recipient that their money has been stopped.

This is a scandal and has left people, quite literally, with no money for food, light and heat.

Want an example and one that caught the eye of national media in 2018? Diane Geraghty, of Lowestoft in Suffolk, was supposed to be receiving £166 a week but the DWP thought she had died - so they stopped her payments. In fact it was her husband who had died and for five weeks she lived on left-over cheese from her husband's funeral until a passer-by – a complete stranger - saw her distress and stepped in to help. Her saviour was David Kinsella, who saw Diane in her garden in obvious difficulty, and arranged emergency food supplies from Lowestoft food bank then contacted the DWP to put things right.

The money Diane Geraghty was supposed to be getting was her old age pension and injury disablement benefit. She is sixty-seven.

You may be one of those who have little sympathy for people on benefits so perhaps it is time for you to stop and think of two things; firstly, are you immune from the possibility that even you might, at some point, need state help to survive, to eat and keep yourself and your home warm in winter? You may believe you are but history tells us that there are huge numbers of seemingly well-off people who suddenly find themselves (and through no fault of their own) without the comforts they had previously. Today's world, even in the UK, can be ruthless in unexpectedly removing entirely what you thought was yours and what you take for granted. The second thought is that no matter how comfortable you may be, if we are to be a serious society and one that looks after its people, you should take care before dismissing one group or another merely because they don't have what you do or at first glance, don't do the things you think they should.

One doesn't have to pray at the altar of altruism or even be particularly generous to think of and act more kindly to those less fortunate - and most people, despite the left-leaning view of equality, are not rich. Or even close to being so.

Back to the DWP – they never have a real person sign their letters. Anonymous 'Decision Makers' with no name hold sway over everybody unfortunate enough to be at their mercy and it is a constant irritant to those who need help that they find it at best, difficult and time-consuming, at worst impossible, to actually speak to a real person. There is a reason for that, albeit an unpalatable one; there have been any number of instances where DWP staff have had to put up with screaming abuse from some of their customers. It does however, take two to tango. If the DWP treated people better, those people might be less inclined to get abusive to start with. In return, DWP staff should be able to do their job without fear. And therein lies the problem.

The DWP takes its lead from its master; the Government. And it is the Government, both Labour and Tory, who give the DWP the leeway to behave as it does. That's the same Government that you elect, the one that is supposed to serve you, the one whose boss you are.

A classic example is that of the 'Work Capability Assessment' (WCA). This is the annual process by which those receiving some kind of sickness benefit (which has had several different names and there are several different types) are sent a substantial form that requires every question to be answered. The form's design phrases the questions in ways that are slanted to get the answer required by the state, not the answer that necessarily tells the whole truth – only part of it. The benefit claimant then has to attend an assessment which is carried out by a nurse (not a Doctor, well-qualified and experienced in the various ills that can befall somebody – just a nurse) who then asks more questions that are again weighted to secure the right answers, and the result is that some very sick people are then deemed capable of working and their benefits are stopped. As mentioned earlier, the first the recipient knows of this is when they go to their bank and find they have no money.

The letter from the DWP, 'signed' by some anonymous decision maker, arrives later. Note by the way, that claimants are not automatically transferred from sickness benefit to job-seeker's allowance so they continue to receive something. Benefits are simply stopped entirely. The claimant has to attend a job centre if there is one or go online and prepare a new claim which means filling in another form and then waiting to be told if they have had their claim accepted. Meanwhile, they still have no money…

The Conservatives are today wholly blamed for the problems surrounding the assessments and Jeremy Corbyn, during his speech to the Labour Party Conference in September 2016, said that that Labour would do away with the, as he put it, 'cruel and inhumane work capability assessments.'

What Corbyn (and others) either don't know or conveniently forget and never mention, is that it was Labour introduced these assessments during their third consecutive term of office.

Not the Tories – Labour. The minister responsible was James Purnell, who resigned before the 2010 General Election that saw David Cameron become Prime Minister, leading the Tory/Liberal Democrat coalition Government (Purnell then joined the BBC on a nice, fat salary, where he remains today).

One of the first things the new Government did was to require all sickness benefit claimants to have another WCA, even those who had passed theirs just a few months earlier. Huge numbers of people, many with terminal illnesses, were then declared 'capable of working' and had their benefits stopped. Some even died. To begin with, the assessments were not materially changed by the Tories, even though Iain Duncan Smith, while Works and Pensions Minister, has been demonised by the left for killing the very ill by taking away their money. In fact, it was Chris Grayling (Transport Minister at the time of writing) who initially took charge of the department after the 2010 election. Such was the furore over the number of people affected that Grayling was moved, Duncan Smith took over and it was on his head that most of the opprobrium fell. His first job however, was to try and make the assessments fairer and less draconian, something for which he has never been given credit.

By the way, since many readers won't know, the assessments work by giving 'points' to each claimant. To receive or continue to receive sickness or disability benefits, the minimum number of points was twelve, the maximum twenty-four. Those who received the maximum, or near it, are placed in a group that defines them as not capable of working and are essentially left alone to carry on getting or waiting for treatment. Those acquiring the minimum or up to around eighteen points, are placed in a second group that requires them to attend regular help sessions that monitors their progress through the illness and is supposed to offer further help to full fitness.

It is this group that has seen the biggest fall in numbers since 2010, not the other one. Put another way, the shirkers who in fact were milking the system, came from this group. The genuinely ill remained in the first group and continue to do so.

Also worth pointing out is that during the 2010/2011 fiasco, the private company carrying out the assessments, the rather inappropriately named ATOS Healthcare, took the desire of the new coalition Government to look again at claimants literally. People went from having somewhere between eighteen and twenty-four points to zero points, which is why very ill people were denied benefits.

Clearly such a drop in points had no credibility. Had such assessments gone from, say, eighteen points to nine or ten, there might possibly have been a viable case. But when somebody with a diagnosis of cancer, or a clearly recognized mental health disability and thus is receipt of a higher points total is suddenly re-assessed and given no points at all, the message had obviously gone awry somewhere. David Cameron's coalition had stated a desire to reduce the welfare bill, not by itself necessarily a bad thing as it needed some reforming work. As in so many areas however, it is how that was done that caused the problem.

In an interview at the start of well-deserved bad publicity, Chris Grayling stated categorically that there were no reduction targets and no incentives to get the sickness benefit cost down; only that the DWP had been asked to look again at all assessments, including those carried out very recently as well as those from a year before.

How did the DWP interpret that? And how did the DWP transmit it to ATOS Healthcare? Nobody knows. Or if they do, they aren't saying. What is undoubtedly as clear as crystal however, is that ATOS Healthcare, wanting to keep their lucrative contract and wherever the ultimate responsibility may lie, were utterly ruthless in subjecting a large number of very sick people to penury, starvation and in some cases, death.

Both the Labour party and the Conservative party must take their share of the blame and what is also undeniable is that such an abuse of power is not the hallmark of a society that cares for its people. Neither is it the hallmark of a free and democratic society.

One of the other things the coalition Government did under David Cameron and Chancellor George Osborne (often caustically referred to as 'Rich-Boy Osbo'), was to freeze the amount of benefits paid.

That the UK was spending too much on everything and not bringing in enough money to pay its way was undeniable. Something needed to be done. Osborne's predecessor as Chancellor, Gordon Brown, was often hailed as one of the best Chancellors the country has had, but the reality was somewhat different and when Brown succeeded Blair as Prime Minister, he had, in effect, made huge numbers of people reliant on benefits of one kind or another. That reliance was due to Brown allowing the cost of living to carry on rising and adding extra benefits to cover it while keeping wages down. Brown of course, was not and is not the only politician to have done so but doing this was nothing more than a naked grab to retain power; by turning Britain into what amounted to a 'client-state', under Labour the UK had run up a huge debt, and the Government of Cameron and Osborne clearly had a duty to try and do something about it. As always however, how it was done caused enormous problems for ordinary people and one of them was (and remains today) the ever-spiralling cost of simply staying alive. Benefit recipients have found themselves without enough money to buy food, keep their home warm in winter and in some cases, unable to have a home at all.

It is to the eternal discredit of both David Cameron and George Osborne that this was allowed to happen and both deserved the criticisms that were aimed at them, to the point where one has to question their suitability to have become MPs to begin with, never mind the holders of the highest offices in the land.

One of Osborne's bright ideas concerned the still-ongoing introduction of Universal Credit, the combining of the confusing multitude of benefits brought about by Gordon Brown's tenure, into one single monthly payment. Universal Credit is actually not a bad idea and was the brainchild of Ian Duncan Smith while he was the Minister responsible. The difficulty for those receiving it is the change from getting one's money every two weeks to getting it every four weeks or every month; there is that extra period to cover. By itself however, it is not an insurmountable difficulty (although it is hard – very hard). Osborne however, made it far, far worse by adding an extra week for 'administration' and then, on top of that…another week, apparently just for the sake of it.

Why?

Why do something that will, and does, mean that a benefit recipient has to go without any money *at all*, for four weeks?

Duncan Smith railed against this arbitrary move and it is one of the reasons why he and Osborne were known not to get on with each other; indeed Duncan Smith resigned as Minister, rather than have his reputation dragged further through the mud by Osborne. It is to the credit of the present Government that the extra week was subsequently removed from the equation but – the additional 'administration' week remains, meaning people will still have a minimum of three weeks without any money.

George Osborne was manifestly unfit to be an MP at all and his time as Chancellor was due to being a Cameron crony rather than having any real ability to do the job. His unfitness has been amply demonstrated by his behaviour since leaving office and Parliament is a better place without him (the same can be said about a number of other former and current occupants of the House of Commons).

Would it have been different under Labour? Would it *be* any different under Labour now? No is the short answer. Blair and Brown, along with the rest of their colleagues, had already shown themselves to be woefully inept at running the country's finances and the spend, spend, spend policies of Jeremy Corbyn and John McDonnell would be undoubtedly worse.

Look at it from a more personal point of view; you have a finite amount of money coming in each week or each month. You might well have an overdraft at your bank to help you get by, but whether you do or not, you still have to spend no more than you have coming in. Its called balancing your own personal books, managing your money properly. You still need to have enough money to cover your needs however, but where does that money come from?

This same principle applies to the UK and every other country. All have to live within their means. So why does the UK give away billions of taxpayers money – money that *you* hand over to the people that *you* are in charge of – in overseas aid?

That money should be spent here, on our needs first. When we are in good shape, then we can help others. There are times when we should help elsewhere, instances of real need (after a natural disaster for example). We must help where it is genuinely needed, if we are to call ourselves civilised and *if* we can. Helping other countries however, does *not* allow grandstanding politicians to run around the globe showing what great world statesmen they are, as is currently the case. This is why the UK has such a bloated overseas aid budget. It allowed first Blair, then Brown, then Cameron and yes, Theresa May as well, to look good around the world, to show themselves as 'great leaders'.

'Notice me!...I am the Prime Minister of the United Kingdom and my munificence is magnificent!'

We have our own poor to help, our own hospitals to take care of, our own sick people to care for, our own schools to give money to and our own unemployed to look after. When we can do all that we need to here – then we can help others.

Above all, it is time that all political parties told the truth about unemployment; in today's technologically advanced world, where machines can operate more efficiently than humans ever could, no

Government can guarantee that everybody will have a job.
  There will always be a large number, and an ever-growing, ever-
increasing number of people who, whether they want to or not, will
not have a job and we have an obligation to look after them.

9 The Death of Wisdom

You don't stop playing because you grow old; you grow old because you stop playing

George Bernard Shaw (and Janet Clough to me - KJ)

The phrase has become well-worn now. Used almost without thought by every politician and in very nearly every form of news reporting and with great frequency, it is a phrase of three words that should be of huge concern.

Those three words are, 'An ageing population...'

In case it had escaped your attention, let's state the obvious; there are three stages of life. The first is birth. Without that, there is no life. The second stage is life itself and the third is death. The first and third are the most natural in existence and they are an unchangeable given – they have to be so. Only the middle bit can be a little unpredictable.

Yet there is no escape from any of them. We will be born, we will live and we will die. That middle part can sometimes be tragically short. It can also be remarkably long. Whatever its length, one unavoidable, unalterable, unswerving ever-present fact remains; once born, we are all heading in the same direction.

For some, growing older can bring a number of age-related conditions - things don't work as well as they once did. For others, all growing older means is a little slowing down and not running a mile in four minutes any more. But otherwise, age is not something that can or should determine or define anybody. Put another way, if you 'think' old, you will be 'old'. My Mother had something of an obsession about it. She steadfastly refused to give way to advancing years and carried on doing more or less what she had always done. The 'traditional' age for a man used to be three score years and ten, or seventy-one years of age. When he got there, my Father said to my Mother, 'I made it! Three score years and ten - I am now officially old!' My Mother went berserk.

'You are not old!' she screeched. Even though they had been divorced for years but had still remained good friends, Dad had by then learned not to argue and just smiled, nodded and said, 'I'm not? Oh. Alright then.' (and promptly had a diagnosis of terminal cancer confirmed. Mum was not too far behind him with the same).

I beg to disagree with my Mother, at least in part. Although she meant well, anybody aged seventy or over is still getting on a bit. Only a bit mind, as she was however, in one sense, right. What my

Mother was driving at was that merely because one's chronological clock ticks on, it doesn't mean you have to give up living. Or that you have to stop doing things that you always did. Granted you might do them a bit slower but you still do them. It is why, when I am ninety or more, I will be found jumping off mountains, hang-gliding, parachuting, skateboarding and generally behaving like a probably slightly senile and senior delinquent. I will be happy if people do not say, 'What a nice old chap...' but rather roll their eyes and groan, 'Oh hell, what's he up to now?'

There is a wonderful, and true, story about a veteran of World War II, at the time living in a south coast old people's home and in his nineties, who wanted to attend the war's anniversary celebrations across the Channel in France. He was told by those running the home that he could not go as he was too old for the journey.

So he went anyway.

He was duly missed and was reported as missing. A search took place, somebody remembered his desire to go to France, and there he was. When asked why he did it, his reply was that he was quite capable of doing it, so he did. He wasn't going to be ordered about. There are other examples and quite a few of them. In the news recently was a man who celebrated reaching 100 by going parachuting; he had done the same on his eightieth and ninetieth birthdays. Others do similar things frequently. Such an attitude is not unusual and can be found around the world. In many countries, older people are revered, they are listened to and when needed, looked after and cared for. Their life experience is considered valuable.

Except in one – this one.

The United Kingdom has gone out of its way to drive a wedge between generations. It manifests itself in a number of ways, most notably the way in which older people are left to rot in hospital corridors or denied the basics of dignity in some outwardly respectable yet ill-named 'care' home - and also in those three words, 'An ageing population.' By using them so often and in such a throwaway manner, politicians are, in effect, saying to those who haven't yet become more mature, that older people don't matter and they are causing the rest of society a problem. The old are a nuisance and we need to find a way of getting rid of them.

Remember Logan's Run? It may not yet be tied up at the dockside, or perhaps not even in the harbour, but it is offshore and waiting to be invited in. Perhaps those who say, 'an ageing population' so casually might care to remember the three stages of life and that they too, one day, will wake up one morning to find a wrinkle that wasn't there before, a strand of grey that they didn't have before...and yet another birthday has been and gone.

The Death Of Wisdom

So why has it happened? How did it happen? Is it possible to find a moment, a period of time, in which this ideology really took hold? Is it possible to do something about it? There is an answer to the first three questions. The fourth? Maybe. But it will take a sea change in attitude to find the right one. I live in hope – no matter how many mountains I leap off, I too will get old one day.

The when was 1997; the year Tony Blair became Prime Minister. Blair was a departure from the way Prime Ministers looked and behaved. Until 1997, a Prime Minister was a mature figure, with some years behind him (her in one case). Most established politicians looked pretty much the same in that sense. They were people who had been around the block a few times, they had done things and been somewhere. They had some wrinkles and a little, or even a lot, of grey hair. Some of the men didn't even have hair anymore. It is one of the reasons why many younger people, having reached adult age, tended not to vote; that was something they could do later in life, when they got a bit older – they were still having fun and loving being young. Getting older and mature (and voting) would come around when it came around. But those younger people still had some regard for those older than them, in some cases much older. How many, even while still at school, had a mature man or woman as a friend or neighbour? Most of them. How many would go and see them for a bit of advice on something that their youthful minds wrestled with and that they would rather not talk to their parents or peers about? Quite a few. More in fact than was often realised – and how many of them came to some kind of harm because they had some association with an older person? Very few. Most younger people benefited enormously from being able to speak to and associate with (even to a limited degree) older people.

Tony Blair changed all that. He was, for a Prime Minister, or for that matter any politician, very youthful. He had a winsome smile, not a wrinkle anywhere and a full head of lush dark hair. He bounced around grinning at everybody and took his jacket off at every opportunity, showing how informal he was, how approachable he was. He kept his tie on but, hey! No jacket! PM's never did that. Most of all, Blair was, allegedly at least and as he himself once infamously put it, 'A pretty straight kinda guy.'

He went out of his way to associate with those admired by young people and children. He entertained pop stars. He invented Cool Britannia...

Blair was also, and still is, a Euro-fan. He did in Europe as he did in the UK, beaming his way around the EU and one of the side effects of Blairism is the way in which other countries' leaders suddenly started looking much younger. In the UK, the Conservatives had William Hague and Iain Duncan Smith as the party's leaders. Neither was 'old' but neither had a full head of hair either. That wasn't cool. The Tories wanted a Blair. So they got David Cameron... The Liberal Democrats had Sir Menzies Campbell, former Olympian and a man of great experience and quite a bit of know-how. But boy, was he old...he looked (and sounded) a little doddery from time to time. He wasn't, far from it in fact - but he looked it. He was another one who didn't have any hair . So the Lib-Dems turfed him out and got Nick Clegg...

When Cameron and Clegg became Prime Minister and Deputy PM of the 2010-elected coalition, they were often seen touring around hospitals and other places minus their jackets. *'Hey look! We don't got no jackets on bro'...Blair did that so we are too coz we're cool...but get this – we took our ties off AS WELL! How cool are we?'*

Both simply looked like two half-dressed, scruffy, middle-aged men trying to be trendy and failing miserably.

If you really want to be a serious politician, keep your jackets and ties on

As Blair bounded around being youthful and cool, it was the time when politicians (no matter what they looked like) began to insert the words 'Young People' into every second sentence. But it needed more than mere words. So under New Labour, new laws came in and by the bucketload. And the most significant of them were designed to cement Blair, New Labour and the young as tightly together as possible.

If you want to control people, there are two ways of doing it; the first is by being blatant and obvious, by using force and intimidation. That doesn't work too well in a country like the UK (for the most part at least, and...not yet) so the second is more subtle; by instilling fear. Of what doesn't really matter. Just instil fear. The terrorist atrocities of 911 in the USA gave Blair the perfect opportunity. He swept across the Atlantic to stand shoulder to shoulder with America, basking in the applause when President George W. Bush, addressing the combined houses of US Government, turned to look at the country's quickest and first guest after the attacks, saying, 'Thank you for coming friend'.

One could almost warm one's hands on the glow of self-imposed importance as Blair sat there, drinking in the standing ovation granted from the highest of American high. Both in the US and the UK, everybody said, *'Wow...what a guy...a pretty straight kinda guy...Cool Britannia...'*

Blair could do more or less as he pleased. His Government had a sweeping majority in the House of Commons and his new laws were passed with little opposition. Except...except, except, except...

Tony Blair never really had majority of people voting for him and New Labour. If one looks carefully at voter turn-out for all three of the elections held while Blair was Prime Minister, it was very low compared to previous elections. And the young still tended not to vote too much. So some of Blair's laws were targeted at older people, most of whom still knew their history, still had knowledge of Communism, Marxism, two world wars, and the abject failures of Labour Governments to manage taxpayer's money properly - and most of those tended to vote Conservative. They weren't Labour voters. So they didn't matter.

Tony Blair had two over-riding objectives; the first was the advancement and enrichment of Tony Blair (amply demonstrated by his money-grabbing behaviour after leaving office) and the second was to beat Margaret Thatcher's eleven years as the country's Prime Minister. Having discounted the older voter it meant targeting the young, but to do that meant achieving the second aim, thus giving kids a chance to grow up and get to eighteen.

So Blair's laws began to instil fear; fear of the terrorist - and fear of the old. The old were stuck in their ways, would not change so didn't matter and they were probably all paedos anyway. Blair's laws ruthlessly homed in on child protection, run up to that point by an admittedly under-funded, understated but admirably decent set of organisations. All went about doing their job well with little fuss *and* without setting people against each other. Blair's Government handed sweeping new powers to them and turned child protection into a massive industry of itself, with anybody over a certain age targeted.

If somebody was fourteen in 1997, they reached eighteen, and could thus vote, only four years later and could then vote at the second election won by Tony Blair. By 2007, such young people had got to twenty-four and by 2017, at thirty-four, are in many cases now parents themselves and are bringing their children up with the same fears they had imposed upon on them as teenagers. To their eternal discredit, the Conservatives, since 2010, have done nothing to redress the balance. Is that a surprise? David Cameron (and Nick Clegg) were just as ageist as Blair had been, and being young and funky is what matters. Being old is bad.

The curious part to all this is that while it did work, it didn't work quite as planned. Blair never managed to beat Thatcher's record and the mass turnout of the younger voter wasn't quite the mass turnout as planned either.

Possibly one of the most perfect illustrations of the political bias against older people is the insidious suggestion by Lord Willetts, once known as Conservative MP and Minister David Willetts, of giving £10,000 to all those young people reaching the age of twenty-five (The Institute for Public Policy Research also made the same suggestion a month before Willetts – he however, has a higher public profile).

Willetts is, at the time of writing, the Executive Chairman of the

Resolution Foundation's Intergenerational Commission, and was known as 'Two-Brains', apparently due to his allegedly high intellect. If he is as intelligent as he is supposed to be, then the suggestion of giving away a free £10,000 to people simply because they are young and get to a certain birthday can only be interpreted as a deliberate attempt to further alienate the young from the old. Particularly since it will be paid for by increasing taxes, in one way or another, on older people.

Yet Willetts is hardly young himself. Just as he was while an MP, he is bald and has wrinkles. So why has he come up with this divisive idea?

David Willetts was the Minister for Universities responsible for putting tuition fees up from some £3,000 to £9,000 while in office (see later for who actually introduced them to start with). Let us leave aside the numbers now in Parliament who never had to worry about such fees because they didn't exist when they went to University – this £10k is apparently to help those aged twenty-five to get on the property ladder as few of them can now afford to buy a home (again, see later), set up businesses, invest in their pensions and…to pay for education.

University Tuition Fees - £9,000. Free cash at twenty-five - £10,000.

Go figure.

Are people really that stupid? £10,000 isn't going to cover those University fees; they are £9,000 per year, *not* just nine grand all in and covering the four years one might attend a university (including a gap year). This is why graduates end up with a debt of £30,000 before they have even started a job. £10k is simply a gimmick that is a play on perception. By the way, as a slight aside, isn't it interesting to note that as soon as the higher fees came into force, Universities immediately jacked up the salaries of those who run them.

Just a thought…

The divisions between generations that exist now have little or nothing to do with any supposed injustice or imbalance between young people, and those now old enough to have bought their homes and who are supposedly getting wealthier at the expense of the young. Those divisions exist because of the way in which older people have been demonized by politicians of all colours and who propagate this by the things they say, like 'An ageing population'. People like Liberal Democrat leader Vince Cable, who said after the EU referendum, 'The young have been shafted by the old.'

Cable is another ageing, bald oldie – he was seventy-five in 2018.

Such comments, such ideas, are designed to show how 'in touch' these monuments to political shallowness and self-preservation are; they are designed to tell the young that these decades-old luminaries 'understand' and if you are 'young' then you really ought to vote for them as only they really care.

No they don't. They are interested only in themselves, their superior status along with their power, and not in you, no matter what your age.

Blair's targeting of the young has also manifested itself in less obvious ways, but most especially in people who went to secondary school during the Blair years. As said already, all are now in their mid-thirties and may well have young children themselves; those who are now parents of young people in their middle to later teenage years will have been young adults in their early twenties in 1997 and, undoubtedly carried along by Blair mania, many of them (not all however) show a marked lack of thought and consideration towards others. That has been passed on to their sons and daughters. Unintentionally perhaps, but nonetheless it shows up in the attitude of many of the young towards the old.

Twenty-one years on from 1997 - a public backlash arose as a result of a vulnerable woman, aged forty-nine, who was pelted with eggs and flour by six teenagers aged between fifteen and seventeen in a park in Bury St. Edmunds. A photograph of the incident, which took place on Friday 27 July, 2018, was posted on social media by one of the teenagers and quickly went viral. By Tuesday 31 July, just four days later, the teenagers had been named and shamed on social media platforms and the resulting threats to them meant their parents asked for Police protection.

Why did they do it? In all probability it was simple, unthinking behaviour that, to the teenagers, was nothing more than a bit of fun, having a go at somebody 'old'. The real question however, is why that attitude was present to begin with. The stepmother of one of the seventeen-year-olds was quoted as saying that he was a good lad who had never been in any trouble, adding, 'He's not a tearaway, he's just a stupid boy.' The assessment is, again in all probability, correct. Teenagers have always been prone to doing stupid things but it is only in recent times that such stupidity has manifested itself in direct (or indirect) assaults of one kind or another, on older members of society. And the responsibility for that lies with their parents, like so many today, the products of Blairism

I am sure that these teenager's parents are not 'bad' parents. I'm equally sure that the teens themselves are now genuinely sorry about the incident - but their parents have not brought their sons up to be respectful of others and especially of those older than them. Put another way, they simply don't think.

The threats made to the teenagers are not the answer and are nothing more than revenge. As we have already seen earlier in this book, revenge is not justice but it seems to me that little will be gained by making criminals of the boys involved. Perhaps a more appropriate course of action would be, since their identities are now well-known (particularly in Bury St. Edmunds), for them to publicly apologise to the woman and do something practical for her to make up for their unthinking behaviour. That may sound 'soft' but unless any of them already have records, or come from families that are 'known' to the police (in which case let justice be exemplary), again as we have seen earlier, being criminalised for being stupid is not the answer.

Putting right the damage of Blairism is.

There are other examples, many less obvious than that of thought for others. The Chief Executive of the Royal Academy, Charles Saumarez Smith, has suggested that museums and galleries are trying so hard to attract the young that they are ignoring older visitors. At the 2018 Hay Festival, Mr Saumarez Smith said that even his own institution has bowed to what he described as the 'ageist' trend of valuing the young over the old.

On such accusations of ageism, at the beginning of June 2018, Tory MP Andrew Bridgen was quoted in a national newspaper thus; 'What Mr Saumarez Smith is saying might not be trendy or politically correct but it's the absolute truth. We do have an ageing population, wisdom comes with age and we need to value all our citizens equally.'

Even though he undoubtedly meant well, Bridgen still fell into the same trap as so many of his parliamentary colleagues, those same politicians, of all shades, shapes and sizes, continuing to parrot that now worn-out phrase, 'An ageing population' as the root cause of the country's ills. Bridgen should have chosen his words more thoughtfully, perhaps saying, '…we have a population made up of all ages and as people grow older, wisdom comes with age…etc.'

The steady drip-drip-drip of age bias inevitably filters its way down the chain. Letters in national newspapers can be quite revealing and one featured the following comments:

> Families are expensive to the state and the taxpayer. Increased longevity is a growing burden.

The letter writer was from Newmarket, in Suffolk. Leaving aside the remark about families being expensive to the state and taxpayer (why should this be so? It is another story altogether), the second sentence is remarkable: 'Increased longevity is a growing burden.' What does this mean? Think about it for a moment…*Increased longevity is a growing burden.*

A burden? A load to be carried? Something that is exacting, oppressive and difficult to bear? A burden – something that is onerous. The statement means that the longer we live, the more it costs to have the old around; it means that those above a certain age are worthless and a strain on the rest of society.

It means an ageing population is to blame for the NHS and its

The Death Of Wisdom

inefficiencies and the NHS denies certain treatment to certain people because they are old and its not worth the expense – give help to the young instead, they will be around longer. An ageing population was to blame for Brexit. An ageing population is to blame for paedophilia. An ageing population is to blame for terrorism (those behind it and sending their young to die are after all, quite old). An ageing population is to blame when it rains too much or the sun shines too brightly. So the old continue to be left abandoned in hospitals and homes. Young people are told to stay away from older people because they are old and thus they are dangerous; *berate them! Castigate them! They are old!...eggs and flour!* The mature, like Diane Geraghty, aged seventy-six, of Lowestoft, abandoned by the state and its agents because *she is old!* That passer-by, the complete stranger, who saved her; David Kinsella – he is sixty-seven.

Would a 'young person' do what David Kinsella did? Fortunately, yes. There are a number of examples of younger people bucking the trend and going against the will of the state and its agents and befriending older people. They are however, not the majority yet.

So all that knowledge, all that experience (good and bad), all that wisdom, goes to waste.

Yes, including that of those such as David Willetts and Vince Cable, even if it is only how not to do it as they are perfect examples of the self-serving members of the elite ruling class. Yet it does not have to be this way. Having quoted one letter from a national newspaper, this one makes enlightening reading:

> It's unfair to accuse the older generation of intolerance *(referring to previous letters).* Young people and 'oldies' should learn from one another. We need tolerance and respect on both sides.
>
> Listening is a rare virtue in these days of manic activity. Young people bring energy and much-needed fun into older lives, while the older generation can offer the wisdom of lessons learned.
>
> Both generations can benefit from shared experiences. If we can find common ground by understanding our differences, it will be a better world for all of us.

The letter was written by a lady from Mansfield Woodhouse in Nottinghamshire. She may well be in a minority right now but if the savagery of Blair's legacy can be countered, there may be hope for those in the UK as they get older.

It is however, that common ground referred to by the lady of Mansfield Woodhouse that is the biggest curiosity. It is so because, despite the inevitability of each passing birthday, the remorseless passage of time, nobody, not a single politician, not a single voter, not a single teenager and not a single pensioner, not a single newspaper, not a single internet blogger has spoken up (except me), and said, 'No matter how young you are now, no matter how cool you may be now…YOU…will get old one day.

You cannot avoid it, you cannot change it. You WILL get old one day - including the letter writer of Newmarket in Suffolk and the boys of Bury St. Edmunds.

Unless…(and except for politicians, who are exempt)…

Logan's Run is coming.

10 The Orwellian Enigma of Subtle Oppression

One of the penalties for refusing to participate in politics is that you end up being governed by your inferiors.

Plato

This used to be a free country. Allegedly it still is. Allegedly – but we Brits have meekly surrendered many of our freedoms. Among those are the freedom to be an individual and the freedom to make a mistake and without being criminalised for it.

We think we are free but we're not. Since 1997, when Tony Blair conned his way to power, three things have been used, and often with ruthless stealth, to erode and remove freedom. Terrorism or the threat of it is one. Paedophilia the second and the third is Health. Most people, even now, still don't buy the idea that every day we are going to be blown up. As a nation, we've been there before. Hitler's bombs didn't make us cower. The IRA's bombs didn't make us give in. Terrorism today hasn't either. So we think we are standing up to them. But we're not. We meekly allow the state, our government, to use the threat to remove our freedoms.

A Tourist made to delete photos on his camera of a bus station in London; in case he might be a terrorist. Another made to delete photos of a chip shop; in case he might be a terrorist – and yes I'm serious, it actually happened…a chip shop! Really… Aviation enthusiasts banned from watching airliners at the airport; in case they might be terrorists. At, of all places, the Labour Party conference, a heckler, a party member for decades and from immigrant stock since arriving in this country even before that, and thus an OAP, removed by Police using Anti-terrorism laws, brought in by the same party that was in government at the time - Blair's New Labour.

But the Tories are no better - currently anyway. This is the Tory Government that brought in a measure that gives the taxman (a.k.a. Her Majesty's Revenue & Customs), the power to raid an individual's bank account - in case the person concerned might be a tax-evader. This is also the Tory Government that has imposed further surveillance on the people, giving the state the right to pry into our emails and electronic communications, on the basis that somebody 'might' do something wrong.

Those who vote Labour because 'they always have' aren't thinking.

They aren't looking with any care at what New Labour did. Labour now is, apparently, not 'new' Labour anymore. But the people behind Blair, and Brown, most are all still there. People like Harriet Harman and others. Some have gone, and many are now on the back benches since Jeremy Corbyn became leader of the party but the principles behind New Labour are all still there. Waiting to impose their will, by whatever means are needed, on the unthinking masses.

From Arthur Miller's 1953 play, *The Crucible*, comes this line:

> 'We are what we always were in Salem, but now the little crazy children are jangling the keys of the kingdom, and common vengeance writes the law!'

Miller's play was about the witch trials in seventeenth-century Massachusetts, USA, but it was also about the anti-communist hysteria during the late 1940s and early 1950s that swept the country under US Senator Joseph McCarthy. Hundreds of people were falsely accused of unpatriotic behaviour yet in many cases the allegations turned out to be either trivial, entirely without substance, or simply made up by people with a grudge. The climate of fear that it created remains to this day, much like the paedophilia hysteria gripping the UK – same principle, different method.

The name of McCarthy however, will always be associated with the persecution and pursuit of individuals for political gain – and in a somewhat more sublime way, it is the way the Labour party behaves. Why would Labour do so? To understand this you have to understand the party's beginnings. The Trades Union movement started Labour. It was their party. Why the recent furore over the Unions influencing Labour policy is a mystery to me. Why should the Unions not have some influence? It's their party - and there's the problem. The Trade Union Movement is actually a good thing. At least in theory it is. Believe it or not, I'm a member of one, by choice and quite freely. Yet it has one inherent flaw.

A union only works if everybody is in it.

An example; A company has 100 employees. Forty are in a union, sixty are not. The union looks after the interests of its forty members. That's what it's for. So who looks after the other sixty? Well…nobody really. But they get the benefit of what the union does. So the union, not unreasonably, takes the view that the sixty should be in it along with the forty. Take pay. It's the usual reason for a dispute. The union wants A. Management offers B. The two cannot agree so the union calls a strike. Forty go out, sixty do not. The employer can keep going. Ultimately the union either gives in or the forty probably get fired. On the other hand, if all 100 are in the union, then whatever the union wants it will probably get. *But what if all 100 don't want to be in the union?* Sorry – you have no choice. If you work here you're in the union whether you want to be in it or not. It was called the Closed Shop and you did what the union told you to do. That isn't freedom. It's not democratic. It's not giving the citizen, the ordinary worker, the choice.

Granted the closed shop isn't around anymore but that inherent flaw can, does, has been and still is, the cause of oppression. And since the Unions started the Labour Party, the same thinking still pervades Labour today. It can only be this way. Otherwise the Labour party is not the Labour party.

Before 1997, Labour had never been in government for more than one term of office. Five years. That's all. Ask yourself why. From 1997 that changed. Labour won three elections in a row. For the first time ever, the party had time to really get to work - and it did. It is in Labour's nature to control. It is hard-wired into its DNA. So control is what matters. To have control means having power. So power must be acquired, kept and used. Which means it is the party of oppression. It can be no other way and under its current leadership, those traits are even more marked in 2017 and 2018.

Yet its supporters cannot see this. They have either been beaten into submission – in the metaphorical sense – or conned. Either way, freedom, *real* freedom, goes.

□

Sunday May 4, 2014; keeping in mind that one should not believe everything that appears in newspapers, particularly the Sunday papers and in those with a political bias (which is most of them), the headline in that day's edition of the Mail on Sunday was interesting.

"Red Ed: We Will <u>Force</u> You to Get Fit" it bellows, Red Ed being then Labour leader Ed Milliband.

Apparently he wanted (had Labour won the election in 2015 and Milliband remained leader and thus become Prime Minister), to bring in a raft of new laws compelling us, as in us the people, *not* to do certain things; smoke, eat food they say is bad for us along with other things, and compelling us *to do* certain opposites, like exercise and eat the food *they* say is good for us.

Since 1997 and as the decade went on, and despite the Conservatives coming to power and 2015 became 2016 became 2017 and then 2018, the people become more subject to the rules imposed upon them, imposed by an elite that has never had a real job, that has never got its hands dirty. Thus the state grows ever more powerful.

□

The UK Supreme Court has blocked the SNP-led Scottish Parliament from implementing what they call 'The Named Person Scheme'. Otherwise known as the 'McStasi Law on children', this is the new law in Scotland that the SNP want to impose on parents; every single child has a state-appointed Guardian.

Which is why it has been called the McStasi law – a state-appointed

Guardian? Are they really serious? Or more to the point are the Scottish people seriously going to let the SNP bring this in? Its one thing to be proud and independent but you won't be under the SNP.

For those who may not know, the Stasi were the East German secret police, in the days when Germany was a divided country. West Germany was the democratic half where freedom ruled and elections were held. East Germany was a Communist stronghold, ruled by dictatorship and elections were not held. The Stasi were notorious for using the state school system to indoctrinate children and actively encouraged family members and neighbours to spy on each other and report 'suspicious activity' to the communist authorities. The UK Supreme Court was stinging in its judgement, likening the law to that of totalitarian regimes like East Germany, pointing out that the first thing dictatorships do is get at the children to separate them from the rest of society and bring them up moulded to their oppressive view.

Think about it; what single organisation has unrestricted access to kids all day every day, access enforced by law and spends each day, of every week, putting information into them? Answer – the State, via the school system - including the UK.

Of course it is the sign of a totalitarian regime; the SNP want Scottish Independence. Of itself that's fine, it is their right to campaign for it but what the SNP do *not* want is anybody else running the country – they are, after all, the only party that wants Scotland to leave the UK. It is also why the party's leader, Nicola Sturgeon, is so keen on staying in the EU, which has the same thinking behind it.

However well-meant such things may well be, the road to hell is paved with good intentions and so on....and the most oppressive dictatorships all say they want the best for their people. Be careful Scotland – let them do it and you will one day regret the time you let yourselves be fooled by the SNP.

By the way – the UK Supreme Court used, amongst other things, the European Human Rights Act to tell the Scottish Parliament to think again. That's the same Human Rights Act that certain people (and newspapers) in the UK want to get rid of...

There are some who do not like to say so but whether one does or not, The United Kingdom is predominately a Christian country that has a long and proud tradition of welcoming people from all other countries and all faiths to it. Its principal language is English.

People who wish to come here from other parts of the world are welcome to do so and are expected to respect the UK's history, traditions and culture, its Laws and to learn our language. The UK's citizens and those entitled to reside here are nevertheless free to follow their faith, their culture and traditions, and to live their lives as they wish, free from undue interference.

Stating the obvious I know but it is what makes the United Kingdom the country that it is. Or at least, the country that it is supposed to be. Is it? We like to think so but the reality is that intolerance and bigotry are today as present as they ever have been. Yet again as it always has been, it is not a majority, but a minority. One can see evidence just by looking if one cares to and having looked, then thinking about it.

Most people in the UK don't really care where somebody comes from or what their faith is, or for that matter, what their skin colour is either. Younger generations are fortunate to have grown up and are growing up, in a place where its okay to be different. Yet at the same time, that viewpoint is tarred by those who have imposed it upon them, rather than allowing the young to formulate it as their own. As I've said above, only the education system has everyday all day access to children and young people and it is their job to put information into and influence those young minds. Yet again – is it? Actually no – it's not.

Both schools and universities are today stuffed full of left-wing ideology and that is the *only* ideology imparted to students. There are thousands of dedicated teachers across the UK, all of whom want to see their students leave school with a decent command of all the subjects they teach; English, Maths, History, Geography and more. All the traditional subjects as well as new ones, but they are hamstrung by the one-sided view of a number of their colleagues and significantly, those in charge. A classic example is the number of Head Teachers that sent out letters and emails to parents attacking Conservative policies in the run-up to the 2017 general election. The National Union of Teachers set up a petition and urged parents to sign it. Such partisanship is, or should be, unacceptable but the aim now is not to send students to university with a well-rounded education but to send them with the seeds of one viewpoint and one alone firmly planted in their young minds. Once at university, their education will be completed and the socialist citizen emerges, ready to take on the evils of any other thinking.

That one-sided view includes *not* teaching students about the consequences of dictatorship, of Marxism, the old Soviet Union and why it ultimately failed. Instead, that single view teaches that those things were good, that utopia is a socialist one, that there is no other way and no other way can be allowed. So we have students at universities today who are completely intolerant of any other point of view; where event speakers are 'no-platformed', in other words, not allowed to speak. They are barred and forbidden. We have universities where students want to tear down ancient statues that have stood almost as long as the university has, simply because the statue represents somebody of whom the ideology disapproves.

There is no discussion, no differing point of view. It is not allowed. We have universities where students are given 'safe spaces' to protect them, rather than allowing and empowering them to challenge and ask questions of what might be wrong or right.

Yet schools and universities are where young minds should be opened up to alternatives, where the idea that somebody either had or has a different outlook, can be discussed and dissected.

An open mind can make up its own mind. A closed mind can't.

One of my Father's colleagues, the late and much-missed Peter McDonagh, went to university at Oxford before seeking a career in broadcasting. His autobiography, *Me and Thirteen Tanks*, published in 2014, relates an incident that happened at the end of his time there:

> There is a footnote to my academic career, one of which I remain deeply ashamed to this very day. We decided, as ex-students, finished with studying, we'd make a little bonfire and set fire to our books.
>
> Within a couple minutes the deed was done and we had a bonfire going outside the houses. Suddenly the voice of an old man, heavily accented and in some apparent pain could be heard behind us as we grinned at the fire.
>
> 'Boys, boys! Vat do you sink you are doing?' said the voice, quietening down as he approached us, but filled with a horror we were already beginning to understand.
>
> 'You must never, never burn books!' he said. 'This is what happens when people burn books!' He clutched at his shirt with bony fingers and yanked up his sleeve. On the inside of his arm there was a crudely numbered fading tattoo. From Auschwitz. He was an Austrian Jew, a retired school teacher. He survived two years of imprisonment at the hands of people who burn books.
>
> We were so, so ashamed.

This incident took place in the late 1960s and history – real history – was still taught in schools, and universities had not developed the myopia prevalent today. How many of that old schoolteacher's modern-day colleagues even know of Auschwitz? Of Belsen, Birkenau and the other concentration camps run by the Nazi party that ruled Germany under a dictatorship that led to the onset of World War II, in which six million people died at the hands of the Nazis, merely because of their faith?

How many of the rabid intolerants in the UK today know that Germany under the Nazis was not a very nice place and that dissent and protest was stamped out?

You had your books burned for disagreeing with the Nazis.

You went to prison for disagreeing with the Nazis. How many of today's left-wing supporters know of the 'old' Russia, when it was known as the USSR, or the Soviet Union for short, and a country where democracy was unknown, and where dissent and protest was again ruthlessly crushed? How many know that freedom of speech and freedom of choice, was unknown and that nobody had the right to own their own home (or anything else)? How many of the statue demolishers and no-platformers know of those times? How many of those who shout down others simply because they think the others are wrong and must not be allowed an opposing point of view, know? Do the members of the Students Union at London's City University know that when they banned the Daily Mail and the Sun newspapers, accusing both of fostering 'fascism and social divisiveness', they were doing what real fascists did in Germany and Italy? Did those who burned newspapers during the 2017 election campaign (tweeting images of them doing so) because those newspapers disagreed with their hero Jeremy Corbyn know that the same thing happened in Nazi controlled Germany in the 1930s, along with the book-burning?

And how many today know that the term Nazi is an acronym, short for the party's full name? In English, the term Nazi was short for the National Socialist German Workers' Party. The letters USSR stood for Union of Soviet Socialist Republics.

Note the use of the same word in both...and note also, that the Labour party is a Socialist party.

Today's Liberal Democrat party is another that in its present form, holds no sway with any view other than its own. This is a party whose leader, Tim Farron MP, resigned after the 2017 election saying that his Christian views made it impossible to lead the party. Farron is a practising Christian whose views are considered to be homophobic. This is neither Liberal nor Democratic. It is the mark of the dictator.

Yet can we rely on the Conservatives to be better, to stand up for the rights of everybody? Provided you let them spy on everything you do, apparently you can.

I wrote earlier that the Internet is a wonderful thing that, like almost everything, can be misused by a minority. And it is, on a daily basis. We know that terrorists use it to spread their own ideological views, encouraging followers to kill anybody who fails to also be a follower. We know that children can be at risk online. Yet most internet users will neither look for nor encounter any illicit material (despite the possibility of an unanticipated and unknown entanglement for which the state will criminalise you). If you do look for something then you may well find it – but you have to look specifically for it first, and often look very hard.

We take for granted that when we write a letter – the old-fashioned 'snail-mail' – that when we post it, it will be delivered and delivered without interference. It will not be opened and only the intended recipient will read it. There exist laws however, that allow the state to intercept your mail, and to open it and look inside. Most commonly it happens when you are sent a birthday gift from abroad, or order something from a supplier based elsewhere. The package will be opened and inspected by UK Customs – I've had it with aviation material sent from the USA. For the most part however, the customs declaration suffices and your mail will go from you or to you, via the Royal Mail to where it is supposed to go and will be opened only by the person whose name is on the front of it.

Its called freedom and the right to privacy.

The internet is no different. Yet the state, the present Government, has given itself the right to examine our emails without let or hindrance. In case we 'might' be planning a terrorist attack. Some internet correspondence can be sent encrypted so that only the recipient can read it and following the mass murder events in London and Manchester early in 2017, then Home Secretary Amber Rudd called for a 'back door' to allow the state to access private electronic communication, which resulted in this comment on facebook:

> Talking of our home secretary, it is even more disconcerting to learn that she wants a back door to gain access to encrypted social media communications.
>
> Well my dear, the problem is that if there is a back door, sooner or later the bad guys will find a way in and exploit it. That will create risk of even more problems such as identity theft, as well as the more obvious problems of people's private conversations getting into the public domain - leaks of commercially or politically sensitive information etc.
>
> Sorry, but you can't have Britain being seen as a good place for the digital economy to develop and prosper, AND have a back door.

The above quote comes from one of my magazine editors and I couldn't have put it better myself (which is why he's an editor and I merely write for him).

The internet does need some work. It does not however, need to be treated differently merely because it is different to that which preceded it and I repeat once again that if we are to be a truly free society then there are risks that we must be prepared to take.

Yet the state's increasing denial of freedom is not limited to the more obvious. It is more subtle than that and often uses a roundabout way to either increase its power or take even more of

The Orwellian Enigma of Subtle Oppression

your money than it does already.

Under this government, from May 2018, a packet of 20 cigarettes will cost a minimum of £8.20 - and most of the price is tax. You may not be a smoker (you may even be very anti-smoking) but do you not think that in a supposedly free country, where the right of the individual to make their own choices comes first, the idea that a government will tax a legal product so heavily is nothing short of legalised theft?

'Okay', I hear you say. *'Give up then'.*

Let's suppose everybody did. *'Great! No more foul personal pollution!'*

Still okay - except....the government then loses a huge amount of tax revenue. So what happens then? Something YOU like, something YOU enjoy, and most importantly, something YOU NEED will get taxed beyond your ability to pay for it. So YOU will be FORCED to give up something. That's what WILL happen - unless YOU do something about it and demand that taxes are more fairly levied. Including the abusively high tax on a packet of cigarettes - and on fuel, amongst other things.

□

Remember 'Red Ed' and his vow to force us to get fit? It seems that increasing personal body weight is not limited to the UK. That too many of us eat too much, exercise too little and have become overweight is undeniable, with great concern placed by politicians on the young (again...child protection is paramount...we must protect the young! From themselves, from their parents, from everybody and from their food!).

So why are kids getting fatter? Could it have something to do with successive governments, both Labour and Tory, selling off school playing fields and placing so much emphasis on academia that physical activity, even in a mild form, has become less important and less so effectively to the point of non-existence?

Local Sports Centres, most built with taxpayers money, were sold off in their thousands in the 1990s and 2000s, to become Leisure Centres, and turned into businesses that pay their way, meaning that instead of being solely for local people to use for sporting activities, they are hired out as wedding reception venues in order to increase their revenue streams.

Oh yes, we *watch* sport but we don't actually *do* sport; doing it is only for the select few, not the rest of us. There are no facilities anymore as they were all sold off by the Governments that have our best interests in mind... Result – we have child obesity and an obesity crisis generally.

When the World Health Organisation vowed to fight child obesity using the same or similar methods to those used against smokers and tobacco several years ago, few people actually paid any attention. The relentless onslaught against tobacco (huge rises in taxes on cigarettes, along with increasingly stringent laws on where one can smoke and complete bans on advertising) has since gained momentum and has offered governments a method for tackling obesity. It seems European children are getting heavier and less active, so health experts say governments should take the lessons from anti-smoking campaigns and increase taxes to combat teenage fat.

One after the other, European countries have implemented restrictive measures on the sale and marketing of pre-packaged food and drinks, in the pursuit of health policies. In other words, plain packaging and increased prices through higher taxes.

Denmark's infamous 'fat tax' was the first of its kind worldwide and probably inspired others, but like so many other grandiose ideas all done for the common good, it also had unintended consequences and was eventually scrapped. Officially the reason was the administrative costs it created. One might ask however, did the problems to border trade it created with neighbouring Germany have something to do with it (those who lived reasonably close were crossing the border to buy the same things in Germany because they were cheaper)? Hungary also introduced its own fat tax, but this was just as much about getting extra money into state coffers as tackling obesity, in a country affected by austerity measures.

Which is the biggest point; Governments are using so-called health taxes simply as a means to increase their own revenue (put another way, stealing more money from their citizens under false pretences).

It is not however only a question of fair taxation, an amount that is reasonable and within people's ability to pay it. In an article for Euractiv news (an online news agency for the EU) Susanne Czech, director general of the European Retail Roundtable (ERTT), a trade group bringing together the CEOs of retail giants such as Tesco, Lidl, Ikea and Marks & Spencer said:

> 'It's incredibly difficult for retailers operating across Europe to know what is prohibited where and restricted in which way,'
>
> Unsurprisingly, most restrictions across Europe are currently applicable to tobacco and alcohol. But it can get trickier for products like medicines sold over-the-counter, which may require a prescription in some countries and not others.
>
> And the restrictions are being applied across more European countries, Czech said, citing a new sugar tax in Spain and a soft drink levy in the UK.
>
> 'Where does it stop, where does it go?' Czech asked. 'We

understand there has to be some restrictions out there in the interest of public health and public order. But we also want to offer choice to consumers. Is chocolate unhealthy? I would say dosage is what matters most'.

Some industry executives are now beginning to worry about a 'slippery slope' of over-regulation across a whole range of consumer goods industries, which is starting to impact on the EU single market.

Which is the real issue; over-regulation and the power of governments to impose their will on people, an imposition that denies freedom - and that includes the freedom to manufacture something that is still legal and put your own brand name and logo on it, which obviously means having the freedom to have colourful cigarette packaging. The current situation in the UK (and Australia, another supposedly 'free' country) is absurd. The so-called plain packaging is anything but plain. Is it really necessary to have the same lurid olive green colour on everything with vivid pictures of rotting body parts all over it? Is it necessary or is it merely desirable? Not to mention having a legal product hidden behind doors. All this has done is push the price up and results in longer queues at shops and stores while a harassed sales person hunts for the pack a customer wants, a hunt that gets more and more difficult since every pack now looks the same, with the brand name in very small lettering, making it difficult to see. One of the results of this by the way, with fewer and fewer real people employed (having been replaced by robots), is that the few remaining and overworked staff end up giving the wrong brand to their customers.

Yet how long will it be before smoking tobacco becomes illegal completely?

It is only a matter of time but as already said, the tax loss to governments will be immense. Nevertheless, it will happen somewhere at some point; taking the long-term view, in Russia, President Putin's health ministry has proposed that anyone born after 2015 will be prevented from buying them. So the current generation of babes still in the arms of their mothers, are, although they do not yet know it, facing a cigarette-free future.

"This goal is absolutely ideologically correct," Nikolai Gerasimenko, of the Russian parliament's health committee, has been quoted as saying.

A complete ban, thus making the manufacture, import, export, sale, possession and use of tobacco products may have some logic to it but once again the question must be asked; is it necessary...or merely desirable? For any government to impose such a measure upon its people is still an oppressive denial of freedom of choice.

There is also something disturbing about the idea of the state making things look the same; enforcing a bland, dull uniformity in which the individual spark of brightness and colour is ruthlessly extinguished. Everything must be harmonised. Everything must be as the ruling elite demand and everything and everybody must be equal (although some are more equal than others...have we not come across this before?)

You may, as I said above, be very anti-smoking. So here's a question; do you like a glass of wine with your Sunday lunch? A six-pack of your favourite with the footy on TV? A glass of scotch before bedtime? All of them? Or any other alcoholic beverage?

In December 2016, a report by Public Health England recommended imposing plain packaging on alcohol products, suggesting they also carry larger health warnings, including photographic warning labels, as they now do on cigarette packs.

As if to reinforce the point about government's desire to compel a supposedly free populace to adhere to their way and no other (and yet again focusing on the young) reports were released in May 2018 concerning the House of Commons Health Select Committee recommending that higher rates of tax should be imposed on 'unhealthy foods as a possible measure to tackle childhood obesity'. Most foods in the UK are not subject to tax other than VAT on junk food at the standard rate of seventeen-and-a-half per cent (some European countries have a higher rate, like France, where sweets and chocolate attract a rate of twenty per cent but healthier foods only five-and-a-half per cent). The select committee also called for the soft, or fizzy, drinks sugar levy – which has resulted in a significant reduction of sales – to be extended to puddings and similar products.

Perhaps it might help if healthier foods didn't cost so much more to begin with.

However, returning to the points raised earlier regarding poor parenting, Mummy and Daddy should take some responsibility as well; there was a wonderfully apt cartoon published in a national newspaper in 2018 which depicted three young children sat around the dinner table, all of whom were rather rotund. Their equally large father was cutting slices of pizza to add to the chips and crisps on the table; behind them, their extraordinarily huge mother entered the room carrying her newly born baby. The caption to the picture read:

'Yoohoo, family! Mummy's home from hospital with our new baby...

...fill her up!'

It is, once more, a question of upbringing on the part of those who bred both the over-sized mother and father shown in the cartoon; there are a number of today's parents who have pre-pubescent children (and for that matter, kids in their early teens also) seen on a daily basis ambling around shops and stores across the UK and who fit the description of those depicted in the newspaper. There is little doubt that the campaigns to do something about obesity are right in the desire to increase health generally as well as have a longer life...except...longer lives will mean yet more *old* people...

Are the numbers of the obese really as bad as they are made out to be? Whilst there is evidence clearly seen in any street on any day, is there not the possibility that there may be a little exaggeration in use, simply to propagate the career politician's view?

Be that as it may possibly be however, it is not the principle that is wrong. As already stated earlier, it is how it is being done that it is the problem. It is the element of compulsion that matters. Another of Ed Milliband's statements while Labour leader was this gem; 'I believe in the power of government.'

What about the power of the people who gave you your job, Ed?

You might well be in agreement over health concerns but the real question is, as Susanne Czech said above, 'Where does it stop, where does it go?'

Yesterday - tobacco; today - alcohol; tomorrow - food; the day after that – who knows? You think you are immune to the state wanting to impose its will on you just because you don't smoke?

You are not.

Maybe you don't smoke or drink alcohol - but there are very, very few people who do neither and on top of both, do not drive a car. Okay, you don't smoke, you don't drink booze (and you don't eat burgers and chips either) – but aren't you a little tired of being taxed to the hilt so you can have the freedom to travel as you please, where you please? Or even just to get to work?

There are many who seem not to realise the threat faced by ordinary people in the UK. Perhaps they don't want to realise. Perhaps some follow the hard-left mantra of there being only one permissible point of view. The National Health Service, covered in the next chapter, is an organisation close to the heart of those on the left and in the Labour party, but the debate over it has led to some remarkable statements; one excellent example was featured on the letters pages of the Daily Mail newspaper, on Monday 16 October, 2017. The writer of the letter said:

> The problems the NHS faces would disappear if we all lived a state-approved lifestyle...

It is indeed, a truly astonishing thing to write and then have published by a national newspaper that leans to the centre right. Assuming the writer does actually believe what they wrote, such a statement can only have come from somebody who is extraordinarily naïve, completely ignorant of history (either by choice or poor education), entirely deluded or who is indelibly and in all probability irretrievably in love with the extreme left.

Earlier in this chapter, I wrote the following: 'The UK's citizens and those entitled to reside here are nevertheless free to follow their faith, their culture and traditions, and to live their lives as they wish, free from undue interference'.

It is those last eleven words that are the most important; *'...to live their lives as they wish, free from undue interference'*.

Who decides what is healthy food and what isn't? You? Or your government, the one that you are supposedly the boss of? The steadily increasing imposition of the will of the state, in every sphere of life, is one that should worry everybody. There is no dispute over the idea that a responsible government should encourage those it serves to live as healthily as possible. However, continual increases in taxes are not the way to do it, particularly while doing nothing to *decrease* the price of healthy living, whether it is what you, as free citizens, choose to eat or how you live your lives generally. Or for that matter what your children are indoctrinated with while at school and university. On top of that, there is once again the question of how those you give their job to respond, if you meekly comply with what they impose upon you. How do they replace the loss of those ever-increasing taxes should everybody give up smoking, drinking alcohol, eating what they choose, and thereafter following, as the letter writer put it, a 'state-approved lifestyle'.

What do they stick a tax on then?

Yes, too many eat too much and of the wrong things, but history shows that the approval of the state for one thing, leads consistently to the requirement for the approval of the state for everything else. Think back to my comments in the first chapter as well as in this one. It is the route of McCarthy, the road to dictatorship and the path to oppression.

Freedom is under threat like never before. George Orwell got it right - he was just a bit early with the date.

■

11 Three Letters

No society can legitimately call itself civilised if a sick person is denied medical aid because of a lack of means

Aneurin Bevan

Am I the only one tired of pygmy politicians blatantly lying every time they open their mouths and telling us that the National Health Service, the NHS, is free at the point of delivery?

It is, yet again, one of those phrases parroted repeatedly by all politicians of every hue and shade and at every opportunity. Labour say the Tories want to scrap the NHS, the Tories say they don't and all of them say it must remain 'free at the point of delivery'.

'Free at the point of delivery'....what does it actually mean? It means that it costs nothing to go and see your General Practitioner, your GP (or 'a' GP), at your local practice. It means that if you are referred by your GP for further consultation and treatment, you can go to the hospital, be seen and eventually treated - hopefully with success. It also means that if you are in an accident, an ambulance will turn up and take you a hospital where again, you will be treated, and again once more hopefully with success - and you will not have to get your credit card, debit card or cash out to pay for it. The NHS however, is not free. It never has been free and it will never *be* free.

The NHS is paid for, in the first instance, by your National Insurance (NI) contributions, which is what NI is supposed to be for. It is your insurance against getting ill. NI contributions however, don't come close to covering the costs of the NHS and haven't done so for years. The rest comes out of your taxes. So you pay for the NHS twice and before you have used it if you need to. Its not such a bad thing; our taxes pay for the Fire Service as well but we hope we never have to use them - but they are there if we do. Some are lucky enough to never need the NHS either but we still have to pay for it. It is there if we do need it, we pay for it to be there and this is why politicians are careful these days to say 'free at the point of delivery'.

Let's look at that again; where precisely *is* the point of delivery? The GP practice; yes. The hospital; yes - but that's it. Isn't it? Where else does one need to go? What other points of delivery are there?

How about your local Chemist? Most people will, at some point, need to see their GP for something and most people, most of the time, will not need to go to hospital. But your GP does not treat you. Your GP can only tell you what he or she thinks is wrong and what to do about it. For most of us, much of the time, that means picking up a prescription, given to you by your GP - which means that there are the two points of delivery for your everyday healthcare; your GP *and* your Chemist.

Have you seen the cost of a prescription in England lately?

The point of delivery is not limited to your GP or hospital. The point of delivery is also your Chemist, your Dentist and your Optician. Two of them will provide the service at no direct cost and then only in the first instance – the initial consultation. If your Doctor says you need something from the Chemist and your pain says you do, you will have to pay something for it. You can have your eyes examined at no cost but nothing else - if your eyes need some help, as in wearing glasses, you will have to pay something for them.

Your dentist (if you can find one that does NHS examinations) will check you out but not for free. There is an NHS charge just to have your mouth looked at and should you need anything doing in there (your teeth will tell you quicker than anything else), you will have to pay something for it. Its £20.60 to be examined, and if you need one single filling, it jumps to £56.30. You *can* have other things done as well for that, like a tooth pulling out (in addition to the filling) but if its just to have your mouth peered into and one single filling is needed, its still £56.30. If you need more than that – it will cost you £244.30. That gets you everything that needs doing; examination, diagnosis of what's wrong, the filling and that pesky pain-inflicting incisor yanking. Crowns, bridges, whatever, it's still £244.30.

The Dentist remains the point of delivery for oral health and £20.60, £56.30 or £244.30 is not free. Oh, and by the way – if there are any pain-relieving drugs or anything else needed to follow up what is done at the Dental surgery, the Dentist will prescribe it for you and its back to the Chemist to get it. Which still has to be paid for.

The NHS is not therefore, free. At the point of delivery or anywhere else (other than the initial chat with doctor or optician) and it is time politicians stopped telling bare-faced lies about it. Its not quite the same in Scotland, Wales and Northern Ireland, but in England you actually pay three times; in NI, in tax and in actually getting something to relieve your pain, be it prescription drugs, dental treatment or glasses so you can see properly. Yes, the NHS does reduce the cost to you but it is still not free - and if you are on an income that takes you out of the net for financial help, the cost of getting what you need to deal with your pain or help you see properly can be and for many people is, beyond their means.

The NHS does offer a chance to get the cost of prescriptions down though; leaflet FP95 is expansively titled *'Save money on NHS prescription charges'*...*'A prescription prepayment certificate (PPC) could save you money on your prescriptions'*.

Who is this leaflet aimed at? As the leaflet says inside, it is only for people who live in England and obviously it is for those who need more than one prescription regularly and over a sustained period of time. Needless to say, there is a catch; as the leaflet helpfully tells you, *'If you need more than 12 prescribed medicines each year, you could save money with a 12 month PPC'*.

Note the word 'could' in there... The alternative to a 12-month PPC is a 3-month one, which again specifies more than three prescribed medicines in those three months.

Put very simply, the NHS wants you to pay up in advance of your getting the medicine to relieve your pain, alleviate your symptoms or whatever the prescription is for, and the PPC scheme is run by...wait for it...the NHS Business Services Authority.

It may just be me and I could be wrong but I had the idea that the NHS was a health care provider – not a business.

However one cares to interpret it, it is still not free, either at the point of delivery or anywhere else. Yet there is more to it than that so, *'Hang on,'* I hear you say. *'I had this done and never paid a dime!'* You probably did. I have as well, and recently. So let's narrow it down a little more. Some personal experience – let's look at my eyesight (forgive the phrase – I couldn't resist it).

I've worn glasses for decades. Like anything else in constant use (including our bodies) glasses will eventually wear out and the frames will need replacing. Over time, our sight will also change. As we get older, that can be for the worse, the most common example being the need to use glasses for reading although otherwise one's sight is fine. In my case, my sight actually improved as I got older so the lens in my glasses also needed changing. I thus went to my optician, an NHS practice, and was duly examined at no cost. I then was able to acquire two new pairs of glasses, frames and lens entirely free, gratis and for nothing via the NHS. So the system did work - in 1996.

I have regular eye check ups (if you don't you should...trust me, you should) and my sight remained the same for a while. Excellent! No problems there and none until 2005. Nine years on my sight was still okay but my glasses, the frames, were getting on and needed replacing. One reason the frames lasted so long was that I also used contact lenses for a while, which I did have to pay for, so the glasses were not used all the time. But nine years is still nine years so they were wearing out by then. Back to my optician...my eyes might be the same but something else *had* changed – the system. Now, I could have the examination free, I could still have the lens free...but not the frames. Those I had to pay for.

Let's go over this again – examination; free. Lens; free.

But not what is needed to put those lens into - the frames. What am I supposed to do, hold the lens in front of my eyes, one in each hand?

What bright spark dreamed that up? What was the Government thinking? *Was* the Government thinking? Why the dramatic change between 1996 and 2005? The answer to the last question is money; the Government wanted to cut costs so reduced the entitlement to eye care. So which Government was this? In 1996, the Tories were in power. By 2005, Labour were and had been since 1997. So which party was it that looked after the NHS and my ability to see properly? Decide for yourself.

Fortunately things have changed somewhat and more in favour of actually having frames as well and in late 2010 I found a I had a problem with my right eye. My Optician found a cataract had formed so referred me for eye surgery. A few weeks later the operation was successfully done and I no longer needed glasses for one eye at least. Six years later, in late 2016, a cataract had formed in the left eye as well so again my optician referred me and the operation was again successfully carried out in February 2017. My sight is now near perfect for ordinary everyday activities so I no longer need glasses except for reading and writing. I got two new pairs of reading glasses from my optician - those *and* the operations on the NHS and at no cost (other than NI and tax). So it does work and better than it did in 2005. The points of delivery was my optician and the hospital that fixed my sight (same one, same surgeon too, for both eyes).

Hang on yet again – which party had been in power since my eyes developed cataracts? Not Labour. By the end of 2010, when I had the first eye diagnosed and dealt with, the Tory-led coalition was running things and when the second eye was done it was just the Tories. So which party did the job for me? Again - you decide.

One more, another experience of my own; the story of Christmas 2015…

Dec 24; early AM; up and last minute shopping, felt like s*** when I got home, condition worsened as day progressed.

Dec 25; spent drifting in between being semi-comatose and resembling the undead.

Dec 26; Helpful and caring neighbour called a paramedic who arrived five minutes later in one of those speedy colourful little estate cars, took one look at my decaying remains and summoned an ambulance which also arrived within five minutes; went to hospital, was prodded, poked, examined, tested and had various things done to me none of which revealed a thing, so having defeated the best that medical science could come up with, was sent home armed to the teeth with various drugs and spent the next week or so stoned out of my mind.

Decided to celebrate Christmas on Julember 37…

In fairness there isn't too much wrong with emergency response teams when there is enough of them. Be in a real accident in the UK and the chances are you will be rescued pretty efficiently and if your life is in danger there's an equally fair chance it will be saved.

Three Letters

Almost inevitably yet once more, there is however, still more to things than my own positive experience of needing something done. Despite the dedication and devotion of most people who work for the NHS, the Fire Service and the Police (even allowing for my reservations written of elsewhere in this book), my involvement with the NHS, dealt with as efficiently as they were at the time, are not to be found across the country. I count myself as being extraordinarily fortunate to be living in a part of the country where the NHS has, until recently, worked quite well (at least up to a point and it does creak quite lot more these days, noticeably so) but elsewhere is a different story. There are large swathes of the UK where cataract operations continue to be rationed to save money; the blind stay blind. There are parts of the UK where the acronym NHS stands for 'No Hope Service'. People can wait for hours, lying in the street in agony after an accident, waiting interminably for an over-stretched and under-staffed ambulance service to respond and show up.

Get sick or have an accident in the wrong part of the country and you have one foot in the grave.

□

The NHS, overall, is undergoing something of a crisis. Yet the problem is not new. In the late 1990s, I was at a sports centre which had as one of its activities, a five-a-side football league and a player was severely injured, suffering a broken leg. The centre staff, although being qualified and able to offer first aid, were limited by Law in what they could do as this was clearly a case for an ambulance and fully qualified medics. So the call was made – attendance was estimated at something over an hour as the nearest available ambulance was some fifty miles away on another call...

Yet next door to the sports centre was the local ambulance station, complete with one fully kitted out and serviceable ambulance inside. Just no crew to use it - and this, at the time of writing, was twenty years ago. Over those almost two decades, neither Labour nor the Conservatives have been able to do what is really needed with the NHS and there is more to it than simply throwing money at it. As illustrated with our injured footballer (and a huge number of others in everyday situations) the NHS is struggling to cope. Under Labour, some hospitals became places where infections became rife as they were dirty and not cleaned properly. Why were they not cleaned properly? There were no cases of hospital infections (and deaths) under the Conservative government that Tony Blair's Labour replaced in 1997. Although the Tories began privatising much of what had previously been state-owned, Blair's Labour took the concept of out-sourcing numerous things and awarding lucrative contracts to private companies to new heights, including contracts for cleaning hospitals. Labour used the money saved by doing so to bring in new contracts for GPs that gave them higher pay yet also enabled them to work fewer hours and home visits by a Doctor have all but disappeared. Labour also closed many hospital wards and cut beds, despite the popular misconception that such closures are all part of the wicked Tories and their savage cuts. The results of Labour's never-mentioned cuts in the 2000s are that today, Accident and Emergency departments (A & E) are horrendously over-stretched.

Labour can brag about how much it cares for you and the NHS as much as it wishes to, and as much as I may be sorry to disavow you of your much cherished aversion to the Tories, the fact remains that both political parties are guilty of mucking things up. It isn't and never has been only a Conservative thing.

If it is not only a case of money, what is it about the NHS that today means either a good service or if you live in the wrong part of the country, an awful one that might (and has been known to) kill you rather than cure you?

Part of the answer lies with population growth. The NHS is still run more or less as it was when it was first designed and created. Yes, there have been some substantial changes in some areas but essentially it is the same now as it has been for more than half a century. It was never designed to handle the pressure of numbers that it now does. Some of those changes have not been for the better either. Years ago, smaller areas had what were termed 'cottage hospitals', small versions of those found in big towns and cities. Those cottage hospitals could do almost as much as a big one. Granted they did have some limits but getting transport to a bigger facility if needed could be done quickly and efficiently. The larger towns and cities often had more than one hospital, many of them able to handle accident and emergencies as well as specialist services, maternity being an obvious one. Reading for example, in the 1970s, although not the biggest town around, still had two major hospitals; The Royal Berkshire, on the eastern side of town and Battle, on the west. It also had Blagrave Hospital, which for a time was for terminally ill patients, and at the other end of life's spectrum, Dellwood Maternity Hospital. That scenario was found up and down the country. Battle Hospital closed in 2005 (which party?) and all services are now concentrated at The Royal Berkshire. Today, half the Battle site is a Tesco supermarket, the other new-build housing. Derby is another; at one time, the Derbyshire Royal Infirmary (DRI), located almost in the centre of Derby, was complemented by the Derby City Hospital, on the western edge of the city. Since 2008, the DRI has been a derelict and abandoned shell and Derby now has just one major hospital, on the site of City and called the Derby Royal Hospital. Which is fine if you live on the western side, but if you live on the eastern edge, it's a very long way to get there, clear across a city big enough to have a population of nearly a quarter of a million people living in it. Again – which political party was running the country in 2005 and 2008?

Today, there will be just one mega-large hospital doing everything and many of them are not located in the best place. That is partly circumstance – few towns and cities had a site central enough and big enough to either rebuild or build new big hospitals to take on the jobs done by smaller hospitals as they were closed and services moved to the larger ones. But why were the smaller ones closed to begin with? Answer - to save money. The thinking was that one massive hospital, with everything under one roof, would be cheaper to run and more efficient than having several spread over a town.

So is it? Given the current state of the NHS, it would appear not. The problem with one very large, extended building on one site, is that it actually costs more to maintain and look after than smaller buildings and sites, even if there are several of them spread around town. Many of the country's major hospitals are not completely new, although there are some, but those that aren't are a combination of older buildings (some by over 100 years) and new structures. They also tend to cover very large areas and maintaining them can cost a seriously large amount of money.

In order to build those new structures and expand the existing ones, in 2000, Labour created Partnerships 2000, a Private Finance Initiative or PFI. Put simply, PFI enabled hospitals to raise a mortgage to support the redevelopment or expansion of their buildings and did so without increasing public debt because PFI liabilities were kept off all departmental balance sheets, thus enabling the Department of Health to get around their spending limits. The result today and again put very simply, is that hospitals now have what amounts to a credit card bill that they are struggling to pay. Since around 70% of the annual cost of running the NHS goes on salaries and wages, it doesn't leave a lot to pay those debts. Or to spend on actually treating people.

So what can be done about it? Obviously to handle a bigger population the NHS has to change its way of operating and be more efficient. It would help if an attitude approaching 'less-is-more' was adopted and a return to smaller hospitals became the way forward, meaning less expenditure on mega-huge sites and buildings; massive mazes in which people (meaning patients) either get lost or collapse with exhaustion after entering these Byzantine creations on the trek to find the department they need.

Hospitals, medical centres and Ambulance services need to be staffed properly, with enough crews to use the vehicles and not have them sitting in a station because there is nobody to drive them. GP services also need a big change; the idea that people only get sick between 9am and 5.30pm Mondays to Fridays has to go and go fast.

If you are going to be a Doctor, then you need to remember that people get ill on Sundays at four in the morning and at other inconvenient times. It means that you might have to work longer hours sometimes and it means you can't pick and choose the times you work, as an increasing number of younger Doctors are doing. Above all, it means you absolutely HAVE to dedicate yourself to the cause of helping sick people get better – if that doesn't suit you, do something else for a living.

That there is a serious shortage of GPs is self-evident and found across the country. Part of the reason for that shortage is many GPs are retiring, either because they have reached that age or they aren't too far away from it and have had enough of the amount of unnecessary work they now have to undertake. Once more it is a combination of things rather than one particular aspect and one of those things that GPs now have put up with is a huge amount of administrative work to do *as well* as treating patients, which is what most of those who become Doctors do so for; to help the ill get better. That administration work comes from two sources; the Government (of both parties) and the army of managers and bureaucrats that the NHS now employs (of whom we shall speak more later). Another reason for the shortage of GPs is that, as mentioned above, there are an increasing number of younger GPs who do not wish to put in the hours their older predecessors did – as I also said above, being a Doctor means doing more than those engaged in other professions might do. This is something those older GPs understood but their younger successors do not.

Both the present government and the Labour party have promised to recruit more GPs. From where? Yet again, becoming a Doctor, and in particular a GP, is perceived by many born, bred and brought up in the UK, as a long, hard, slog with far too many working hours at the end of it - and an enormous financial burden to pay off for years of their working lives once they do eventually qualify. Being a Doctor, of any kind, has never been a simple matter of going to University for three or four years, then ambling straight into a highly-paid nine-to-five job immediately after graduating. It takes a lot longer than that to be able to have the title 'Doctor' before one's name. It is also one of the penalties of the way in which the UK has developed spoken of in earlier chapters; the 'I-want-it-now' attitude that is so prevalent among a significant number of younger people. Too many have the idea that certain aspects of life are beneath them, as witnessed by a young Nurse (white, British) who said, 'I didn't become a Nurse to wipe shitty arses...'

Yes you did – it goes with the territory.

The result of the lack of interest shown in entering the medical profession by those born and educated in the UK is the phenomenal numbers of Doctors, Nurses and other medical staff now employed by the NHS who were born, bred, brought up and educated in foreign countries. However, since the 1950s, the NHS has employed large numbers of people, at all levels, from other countries. Many of those came from Commonwealth countries and those with direct links of one kind or another to the UK and there is a reason for that; too many native-born British people considered front-line NHS work beneath them – they didn't want to empty bedpans and wipe messy bottoms. It is yet another example of the bad attitudes of those who grew up in the 1950s, 1960s and 1970s – which is where that nurse I mentioned got her attitude from; her parents and Grandparents.

Both Labour and Conservative parties have suggested that they will launch huge recruitment drives around the world to 'bring the best' to the UK but there are two immediate problems with this. The first is that such a policy deprives those countries of their most capable people. It begs the question - why is the UK entitled to take the best from elsewhere simply because it has become so inept at educating and training its own?

The second is that the NHS pays well. Yes, front-line staff should be paid more, in return for which nurses can indeed clean soiled rear ends if that's what it takes to care properly for patients. Essentially however, the rate of pay isn't as bad as it is sometimes made out to be. That attracts many of those from other countries, who can earn more in the UK than they can back home. However, because of the money they get, there are a number of them now here (and a number set to rise considerably) ostensibly employed to help the ill get better, who are little more than foreign mercenaries lining their pockets with British taxpayer's gold.

Despite the high number of decent people (no matter from where they may come) who want to do the job properly, the ability of those who simply want to get wealthy is helped by the bureaucrat higher up the chain. Eager to keep their snouts in the trough, the 'suits' present those at the sharp end with numerous edicts and instructions, none of which actually help people get better and only serve to increase the amount of administrative work required from those who should be helping patients – and the minority who are content to get-rich-quick are also equally content to diligently follow each and every procedure. It means they don't get to do too much actual medical work and they don't have to work for too long each day but they do get to keep their generous salaries.

On the assumption that enough people actually wake up to the misuse of the NHS and its resources, by Governments of both parties *and* some of those employed by it, the solutions are relatively simple. They are not easy but they are simple (there is a difference).

The NHS needs to spend its massive budget more wisely. It needs to get smart with money. It needs to stop paying over-the-odds for everything. It needs to ensure that what it pays for medicine is the right amount and not the vastly over-inflated fees currently paid to the drug companies; if something costs £1 for a high street pharmacy to buy and have in store then that's what the NHS should pay.

The NHS needs to learn that it takes only one person to change a light bulb, not a team of hi-viz vest wearing workers, one of whom conducts a risk assessment, one carries the warning signs to put around the busted light, one carries the ladder, one holds the ladder, one holds the bulb and passes it to the one who actually changes it.

It needs to change the discriminatory practices it now indulges in towards certain groups of people, the more mature members of society being only one such group.

By being pro-active instead of reactive, and in all respects and for all groups of society regardless of age or gender, the NHS could save untold amounts of money annually by doing something *before* the event instead of after it.

And yes, it needs to pay *all* its staff properly.

Where however, does that cash come from if the NHS is to remain free, both at all the points of delivery *and* further down the line?

Would anybody really object to another few pounds a month from their salary on NI contributions…*if* that extra money was ring-fenced and legally restricted to ensure use on healthcare? I don't believe they would. Provided of course, that such legal enforcement prevented politicians from raiding it to fund some vanity project - it has been known and not infrequently. Should any do so or even try, the penalties must be draconian, including dismissal as an MP and a spell in prison. Which might seem a little over the top, but think for a moment; you gave them their job, you are their boss and by misusing public funds, they are defrauding you - and since fraud is an offence that merits prison…if the cap fits…

Rather remarkably, since I wrote that originally and the first edition of this book was published, there has now been talk by the Government of doing this very thing – adding an NHS tax.

On July 5, 2018, the NHS celebrated its seventieth birthday. After seven decades, the two main political parties continue to try and outdo each other in persuading voters and taxpayers that they are the party of the NHS.

There is however, one small problem; only half the households in the UK actually pay tax – the rest, for one reason or another, and all entirely legitimately, don't (mostly because they don't earn enough). Regarding my comment above that a little extra might be paid by that half that do pay tax, opinion polls have suggested that some sixty per cent of them would be content to do so. Provided of course, and as I said above, that extra does actually go to the NHS.

In practice, given the amount of money consumed by the NHS and the figure *it* says it needs, this comes to something like £4,000 a year…from each and every taxpayer.

Not such an attractive idea after all. The present government, led by Theresa May, almost became an ex-government as a result of the general election held in 2017, having lost the slender majority it had up to then. One of the reasons cited was the idea that extra funding for the NHS would be paid for by extra taxes on the elderly by taking it from the sale of the homes of those older people who had been receiving long-term care. Jeremy Corbyn dubbed it the 'Dementia tax' and it was almost terminal for Theresa – the suggestion was dropped within days of it being announced.

A few pounds a month is one thing, but a figure of thousands and yet another assault on the more mature members of society, *and* after they have been paying tax, NI and a mortgage all their lives tends to put people off a little.

Naturally, there were, in 2018 as the NHS headed for that birthday, suggestions that the then Health Secretary, Jeremy Hunt, was determined to be able to announce a substantial increase in NHS funding. Labour obviously detests the prospect of the Tories calling themselves the friends of the NHS and (at the time of writing) plan their own big increases in NHS spending - which still has to come from the taxpayer… We have been here before. Under Tony Blair, the massive spending spree on the NHS between 2001 and 2007 was a perfect example of how it should not be done - most of it went on salaries for the suits and higher prices charged by suppliers, *not* treating the sick. Given that the cost of anything always goes up and never down, it is, at least to a degree, inevitable that the NHS will need annual increases in funding from its only source – the taxpayer. But whatever the amount, the government, of whichever party, has a duty to the citizens that made it so (as well as to those who didn't), to ensure that money is spent properly and not wasted – and that includes the staggering amounts spent on health tourists who come to the UK to take advantage of the treatment they can get without paying for it.

As well as ensuring value for money and correct spending, also properly accounting for that spending, there are three further things the Government (the one *you* are in charge of, the one *you* employ) must do.

The first is to educate the young properly, free of ideological distortion and bias, and include the concept that a career in medicine is an honourable one, one that will be amply rewarded both in terms of salaries and otherwise, even though it means a lot of hard work studying and learning first, then working hours of the day not found in other, less demanding professions – and yes, it also means making home visits and wiping mucky backsides. It means actually caring for others. One of the more regrettable aspects of today's society is that members of the medical profession (at all levels) are sometimes abused by some patients; in every GP surgery there are prominent notices informing everybody of a zero-tolerance to such abuse. As right as this is, like the DWP, perhaps if people were actually helped and not fobbed off with some excuse, they might respond better. Put another way; bring respect for others back into fashion (and in every way, in *all* walks of life, not just in healthcare).

The second is to stop trying to score political points off each other and blaming the other side for the ills that have befallen the NHS. Hold your hands up, admit you got it wrong and both Labour and Tory have made a mess of it. Take the NHS out of Government control and have it run by an independent commission, which puts health above and beyond any political consideration. The commission's primary members must be those who know what it takes to run a medical service – Doctors, Surgeons, Nurses, people at the sharp end *and* ordinary people, those who either have or might need, to actually use it. Not politicians or political appointees.

The third is this – bin the bureaucrats. Dump the extravagantly over-paid 'Chief Executives', along with the levels and levels of 'Management' below them. Chief Executives run businesses, not hospitals and healthcare. Medical people run hospitals and healthcare. The bureaucrats see their job as cutting costs, not delivering treatment. They do so by putting as many barriers as possible between the patient and the care needed. They do so by insisting that those who need joint replacement operations endure 'intense and persistent pain' before being allowed their operation (who gets most of these operations – *the old…*). At the same time, those very bureaucrats get six-figure salaries for subjecting people to 'intense and persistent pain'. They dream up 'procedures'. They create forms with boxes on that have to be ticked. Tick enough boxes without actually providing a service that actually helps people get better (so reducing costs) and the bureaucrat can then say. *'Look how many boxes we've ticked! We're doing a great job! Give us more money!'*…most of which then goes in to their well-filled bank accounts. The NHS employs more managers than it does doctors and nurses. Not only that but over the past year, it has taken on yet more of them. The NHS is the largest single employer in Europe and also one of, if not the, most inefficiently run.

Sack the suits and right there the NHS budget would either plummet, or extra cash immediately becomes available to treat patients.

Perhaps I'm being a little naive. Perhaps all the above is a little over-simplistic; but then, history tells us that the simpler things are, the better they work.

·

12 Living

*Again, we find that the space standards of twenty-first century luxury
are below the required minimum for dockworkers in 1962.*

Owen Hatherley

Did you know that I can see into the future? Well, I can. So here's a
little advance notice for you, a glimpse of things to come. I won't put
a specific date or time on this, as it can be changed and changed by
you. If that is, you have a mind to demand that change.

At some point not too far away from now, an army will arise - an
unimaginably large army, numbering millions. A huge number of
people, and an army comprised of men, women, young, old, every
age in between and including children and babies still being carried
by their mothers. Every one of those in this army will be in it not by
choice but because they have been forced to be so. All have the same
thing in common.

They have nowhere to live. They are homeless. All would
otherwise be ordinary people, decent law-abiding people, people
who want to work but cannot have a job because they have no home.
All will have no home for the precise, same and exact reason.

They can't afford one.

No matter what the job they could have pays it is not enough so
they cannot afford to have a home so they have no job. There are
plenty of houses and flats they could move into but all are priced too
highly. The cost of putting a roof over one's head went beyond the
absurd a considerable number of years ago. Recent rises in the price
of a home, both rented and bought, have further pushed the cost
above the ability of people earning the average wage or salary to pay
either.

This has contributed significantly to the ballooning cost of Housing
Benefit and has resulted in the government's efforts to reduce it.
These efforts are entirely understandable but Labour consistently
oppose efforts to do so. Many people criticise the Conservatives for
wanting to get the housing benefit cost to more affordable levels yet
is was the Conservative Party that introduced it to begin with - not
Labour. However, the methods chosen by the present government
and its coalition predecessor, are aimed in the wrong direction and
as is so often the case, results in people at the lower end of the scale
suffering unnecessarily and disproportionately.

One of those methods is the so-called bedroom tax and it must end;
it is not for the state to dictate to people what size home they live in.

What the Government should be doing and the ordinary citizen should be demanding is finding a way to see a sizeable and seriously significant reduction in rents and purchase prices at the *lower* end of the market.

Labour have said that they would re-introduce rent controls but this has two problems; rent controls have been shown not to work in the past, both in the UK and elsewhere and secondly, even if there is a way of doing it successfully, it doesn't address the real problem – the cost of buying a house to begin with. Whether one is buying a house to live in or make available for rent, the plain fact is, they cost too much.

Houses and homes such as the typical two-up-two-down terrace or a 1-2 bed flat should be within reach of everybody, including those on benefits. For example, an ordinary house such as that just described can be found in London, depending on where it is, for sale at prices of upwards of £600,000 *or more*. Rents are usually upwards of £1,000 *per week*. This is beyond parody, particularly when a similar house can be acquired in other parts of the country for less than £20,000.

Do the maths - £1,000 per week is £52,000 a year which is insane

The idea of doing something to not just reduce the price of a house but see the price plummet to previously unseen levels (in comparison to today's wages and salaries) will probably seem a little upsetting to those who already have ownership of a home. Bricks and mortar have always been seen as a barometer of the UK's prosperity but this stance is and again always has been, complete madness. There are many countries around the world where home ownership has never been the norm for many ordinary people and rents are nowhere near the stupidity of those in this country.

Start at the beginning of home ownership; you 'buy' your house. One of the myths around home ownership is that you actually own it. No you don't. Your lender does. You actually own nothing at all. After you pay the first month's mortgage, you might own a tiny bit of one brick but that's it. Obviously as time passes, you get to own more bricks but until that mortgage is paid off completely, you cannot say, *'When I bought my house, I paid £XXX,XXX for it'*. No you didn't. Your lender did.

As a slight aside, one of the curiosities of mortgages is that there are a number of people, and many, many of them, who never borrow money for anything. They stick rigidly to the mantra of *'never a lender or borrower be.'* There is, from the moral standpoint, some worth in this point of view; if you can't afford it, you don't get it until you can. Those that follow this stricture will never entertain the idea of getting a loan for anything. Yet those very same people have no hesitation about getting a mortgage - and a mortgage is the loan of a very large sum of money for you to acquire something that you otherwise could not afford to have. *'Ah but that's different…'*

Why? Because it's called something else? A mortgage is a loan of money - and a loan of money is a loan of money. You are still a borrower being and you still have to pay the money back to whoever loaned it to you.

Another of the absurdities of owning your home is the rise in 'value'. Homes, be they houses or flats, have never dropped in 'value'. Yes, there have been a few periods of time (a very few) when the price of the home you borrowed the money for has gone down to less than the amount you borrowed but such periods have never lasted for very long before rising yet once more. Then rising again, and again. House prices are spoken of as though they are a living, breathing entity, a life-form of themselves and beyond the control of humankind - but they aren't. House prices are entirely an invention of the human species and can be controlled by the human species. So why do they rise so remorselessly?

One word – greed. That's it. Nothing else. Just greed.

Everybody needs somewhere to live. Without that, you have no job and no society. Without somewhere to live you have nothing. Let me give you a little fact, a little snippet of information that you probably never even thought of. Your highly-priced *des-res*, the one you are so proud of going so heavily into debt for and that is now 'worth' so much more than you 'paid' for it, no matter where it is, no matter how 'sought after' the area may be, is actually worth…nothing.

Not a penny. Not a brass farthing, not a dime or a sou. Or even a Euro. Zilch. Nada. Your house is worth diddly-squat. Unless…you sell it with no mortgage or other loan outstanding on it, take the cash and go and live in a tent in a remote field somewhere. There are, as it happens, some who have done just that, or something very similar. Good luck to those that have - but the fact remains that your present house is worth nothing at all because if you do sell it, you still need to find another so you still have somewhere to live - and you are still locked into the same bizarre, mindless upward spiral of house prices. Yes, you may well sell for more than you borrowed, and yes, you may well acquire somewhere else for less and so end up with a tidy little profit but your new place is still obscenely over-priced. You could shrug and say, *'Well okay but I do have that tidy little profit you just mentioned.'* True – you do; and that is where the problem of house prices really lies.

In the movie, *Terminator II,* the character of the youthful resistance leader-to-be, John Connor, sees two small children playing, shooting at each other with toy guns. He says to Arnold Schwarzenegger's terminator (a good guy in the film), 'We're not going to make it, are we?' Mechanically, the terminator replies, 'It is in your nature to destroy yourselves…'

It is also in humanity's nature to be greedy.

That tidy little profit – homes are always talked of as being 'an investment'. No they aren't! Homes are just that; homes. Somewhere for people to live their lives in. They are not profit-making enterprises, the aim being to make money. Having a home to live in is the most basic of basic necessities, along with food, water and the means to clothe yourself and put shoes on your feet.

Because we are greedy, we take something that everybody must have and give free rein to the our worst of ourselves. The law of supply and demand holds that if there is plenty of something and there are plenty of people willing to supply it and plenty of people willing to buy it, the price comes down. That is the nature of the free market. The opposite is also true; if there is not much of something and somebody can corner that something, the price goes up, regardless of how many people want to buy it. House prices shatter the law of supply and demand in every respect.

It is said that there is a shortage of homes in the UK. No there isn't. There is a ludicrous over-abundance of estate agents, the first group after a fast buck for as little work as possible; a group that do more than anybody else to fuel the fires of greed, especially their own. There are plenty of house builders and property developers – the second group who exist in a greed-soaked bubble of avarice. There are mountains of bricks and other materials from which to build homes. There is a good supply of suitable land on which to build homes (and that does *not* include Greenfield sites, other undeveloped countryside *and* floodplains). There are also plenty of people who want homes to buy, to rent, and live in.

That there are too many people in the UK is undeniable but that is not quite the same thing as a shortage of homes and is not directly a cause of a shortage of homes. A significant number of people in the UK should not be here to start with and have no automatic right to be here. An equally significant number are not here permanently and do not need a permanent home; they need only to be accommodated for a short period while they are here before leaving. Neither group includes holidaymakers or other visitors whose stay is even more temporary but take those two groups out of the equation and the number of people in the UK drops dramatically.

Yet if there *is* a shortage of homes, why is there *no* shortage of 'For sale' or 'To let' estate agency boards in every street in every town and village? What there is a shortage of is sensibly-priced homes, both to buy and rent.

When Ed Milliband was Labour party leader, one of the policies he announced was that of seizing land from property developers who had acquired that land to build homes on but were not building any of those homes. Leaving aside my own disquiet at the idea of the state simply taking away private property, one has to ask; why were and are, those who could build more homes on land available for just that not doing so? Why were and are they just holding on to that land without doing anything constructive with it?

Because they are greedy; because at the time of Milliband's announcement, one of those brief periods was under way in which house prices were not rocketing ever upwards, so by not building at the time, developers wanted to wait until the living entity of house prices was going up all by itself and they could then make more money. The period in question by the way was that known as the credit crunch and its worth reminding ourselves of why that happened; greedy bankers are the oft-quoted source and while banks were not entirely free of some responsibility, the downturn started in the USA when two major home lenders got into difficulties because they lent too much money to too many people to buy artificially over-priced homes on mortgages that those people were unable to repay.

It was easier however, to blame it all on the bankers, rather than the real culprit, the insanity of house prices that are grotesquely out of proportion to wages and salaries; prices that are so because of the naked greed of estate agents and property developers.

There is another – yet another – fine example of greed regarding housing and it's a classic; that of Inheritance Tax. As well as a variety of other methods of stealing money legally (legally by dint of the powers it gives itself) from those who have bought their homes, the Government, regardless of party, demands that a huge portion of the 'value' of your home is taken from you when you die. How much is calculated by using that so-called 'value' at the time of death. So, if you bought a house in a good area years ago, when it was 'worth' £XX,XXX, by today, due the already mentioned greed of estate agents, it will now, as you reach your twilight years, be 'worth' a hell of a lot more – and it is that so-called worth the Government uses to work out how much of your money it wants to take from you.

Inheritance Tax is an insidious and plain nasty form of monetary theft from everybody. Given the deranged price of buying a home anywhere these days, by the time the last surviving owner dies (usually the husband or wife) such is the amount of tax now due, that the inheritor – mostly sons and/or daughters – are forced to sell it so they have the cash to pay the tax.

Stop a moment… What if said sons and/or daughters, having long grown up by this time, don't need the original home (in which by the way, they probably grew up, with all the memories of their youth) because they now have their own homes? That is still no cause for the state to take money from them, and most especially since there is a good chance that those same sons and/or daughters now have children of their own – who will need a home when *they* grow up…

Since people tend to live longer these days, the grandkids might already have done so, or at least be close to it. They still need to have somewhere to live however, so they can build their own lives.

There will probably be more than one of the grandchildren and they possibly might want to have their own spaces as they go further in to adulthood but it is only then that the old family home can be sold; to give the grandkids the start they need, the deposit, to buy their first home. Except... There isn't enough left over because of the stupidity of house prices and – the amount of cash the state has taken. It is a tax too far and beyond the ability of people to pay.

Inheritance tax must be completely eradicated. It is not for the state or its agents to forcibly take property and thus money from its citizens, especially when they have worked hard all their lives to have something to pass on to their children and grandchildren.

Pause again...there is yet another group of people unfairly treated by the state because of this hideous tax; there are large numbers of people who are single but are also siblings; brothers and sisters, brother and brother, and most often, sister and sister, who, for whatever reason, stay in their home for life. When one of them dies, the other is not protected by marriage or by the civil partnership act, so find themselves faced with inheritance tax when the first passes on due to old age. The survivor is faced with a massive inheritance tax bill – so has to sell their home to pay it. Which means they then have no home since what is left isn't enough to buy another. So they become a 'burden' on the state, which costs yet more.

But that doesn't matter! *They are old!* So they don't count...

So what can be done about it? Can anything *be* done? Is there any realistic prospect of creating a situation where homes can be available to anybody, including those on low incomes, be those incomes a wage or benefits? If house prices are artificially high, can they be brought down by some kind of reverse action?

All governments have done bad things while in office. But they have also done good things. Even Tony Blair did some good things and so did Margaret Thatcher. Both did numerous things that weren't good but one of Thatcher's good things was the right to buy your home. That of course applied to homes that had been owned by local councils rather than those owned privately. Thatcher's reasoning was simple; firstly, everybody should have the right to own their home and they should have the right not to be ripped off by whoever sold it. That's why council houses were sold at a steep discount, enabling those who did so to buy them. The discounts were able to be put in place because there was no money outstanding on those houses; the costs to councils of building them had been paid off years before through the rents received. The rents they were then getting subsequently was gravy, an endless flow of free money into council coffers. The problem was that councils weren't using that cash to maintain their housing stock; local authorities had become notorious for having council estates that were run-down and badly maintained. Part of that was of course down to residents, but where was the incentive for those who lived on these estates to do their bit when the council seemed incapable (and uninterested) in doing theirs?

Which was the second part of Thatcher's idea; if people bought their homes they would look after them and also be more inclined to do so as they alone would be responsible for them, along with the area in which they lived. It worked. It worked rather well and many of those formerly shabby estates are now clean, tidy and well maintained by those who live there.

But it had its downside and in two aspects particularly. The first was that by placing those former council houses on to the open market, even though one of the conditions was that they could not be re-sold within a set period of time, once that time had expired, their 'value' had rocketed. Those values had done so because of the improvements in the areas overall. At one time, you could not have sold a council house for love, such was the poor reputation of council estates...but now? Now, reaping the benefit of the improved look to an area, buyers were more content to move on to a former council estate. So an ex-council house can sell for as much as any other.

The second was that councils were not allowed to replace the houses that were sold with new ones of their own. Consequently, local authority housing stocks became severely depleted, which is partly why there is the perception of there being a housing shortage now. So what do we do?

As already stated, local authorities had shown themselves to be remarkably poor when it came to looking after and maintaining the homes and estates they owned. Any government owned institution, be it locally owned or state owned, had a deserved reputation for inefficiency and bad management. For the most part deservedly so. 'The Dead Hand of the State' is infamous for its profligacy and ineptitude. That comes down to a poor standard of management in many cases and the inability of local and national government to sack poor workers (at any level). Yet it doesn't have to be so.

Let's try something different...let's look at the world today; in many spheres of everyday life, standards in everything have risen almost beyond recognition in comparison to what they once were. Not everywhere and nowhere near enough to what they need to be but expectations are higher and people are more willing to voice their concerns than they used to. Too many people are still too sheep-like but it is changing. The internet has a lot to do with that as, for those with access to it, they can communicate much more easily and much quicker. Local Councils are more aware of their responsibilities and when they fall short, they can sometimes be quickly and very publicly exposed. So they have become generally more responsive.

Not always however and there are still far too many areas in which standards need to be raised and public accountability still has some way to go but there is a noticeable difference now compared with even a few years ago. You the citizen, the one in charge, the real Boss of the politician and civil servant, also still has some distance to go. It is happening however. So let's take advantage of that. Everybody knows we need more homes but just as local authorities once proved themselves to be utterly abysmal at managing housing, so private developers and estate agents (especially estate agents) have shown themselves to be a bunch of sharks and rip-off merchants who cannot be trusted to provide the homes we need at prices that we can afford. So let's compete with them. Head on and right in their faces.

The government has a duty to not only to defend its citizens, but to look after them, including you. So let it form a National Housing Corporation, or NHC for short (that might already stand for something but I'll use it anyway).

The NHC will not be like state-owned organisations of times past. It will not be subject to the political control of whichever party is in government at time but be independent of it. It will employ professionals, properly qualified and they will either have to perform or be sacked. The purpose of the NHC will be to buy, build, rent, sell, buy back and develop homes. Some of the land (and more than one might realise) that can be used for building new homes is already owned by the state so hand it over to the NHC, at no cost, and out the window goes one of the big set-up costs of the NHC. Land without planning permission for housing is worth very little but once planning permission is granted, greed steps right in and the 'value' shoots up. So *give* the NHC that land. The NHC can also use existing powers to purchase existing homes that are unused as well as build its own (and that's not take or seize unused homes, but buy).

NHC homes can be for single people, couples, small families or large families and every single one will be at the lower end of the price range, within reach of any person, either for rent or purchase. What size of home you want is up to you – it is not for the NHC to dictate to you how many bedrooms you have, its job is only to provide the home you want and can afford. The price or rent of an NHC home will depend on how much you earn rather than an artificial 'market' price, and subject to the whims of greedy estate agents and developers. And it won't matter where in the country NHC homes are; in London, the price will be the same as it is in Land's End, John O'Groats and everywhere in between. If you buy an NHC home, you cannot sell it on the open market but only back to the NHC and for the same price. If you want to buy a bigger home you will do so because you have worked hard and earned the bigger income that brings a bigger home within your reach.

Living

Larger homes are a different matter; once people are genuinely earning enough to buy (or rent) a bigger home then it is up to the individual to decide for themselves whether or not to make such a move and they can do so on the open market. But for most people, the ordinary home should be within their reach – which is the point of the NHC; to make a sensibly priced home truly affordable to all and everybody, rather than the la la land of 'affordable' homes now being created as an artificial condition imposed, mostly by local authorities, on house builders before planning permission is granted (the question must be asked when the term 'affordable' is used currently; affordable to whom? Looking at the price of an 'affordable' home, they are no more affordable than anywhere else).

Having moved in, the responsibility of looking after that home lies with the occupier – not the NHC. Its your home – *you* look after it. Just as you are supposed to if you rent privately; most letting agents (if they are any good) will schedule regular inspections, usually once a year, to make sure that tenants are fulfilling their part of the deal. Did you know that most mortgages also contain the same requirement? Check the small print of your contract to buy. Very few mortgage lenders will follow this up, but remember – you didn't 'buy' your house. Your lender did. So they have a reason to make sure their money is safe and the house isn't going to fall down because you aren't looking after it before you pay off the loan.

As to the concept of the NHC - idealistic? Perhaps. Fantasy? Not really – it has already been done, albeit in a slightly different form and has been for over twenty years. Local authorities, in partnership with the right developers, have been building homes that are rented in the first instance but every month's rent goes towards that home becoming yours. The rent takes the place of the mortgage. There just hasn't been enough development of that kind.

□

The oft-quoted figure of the average wage of £25,000 per year is somewhat misleading. If one takes the higher-end salaries, and then the lowest-end, one does indeed arrive at a figure of around £25,000. However, most people do not earn anywhere close to the kind of sums earned by the top earners. To find the *real* average wage earned by real average people one need only look in any jobs section of any newspaper. There is no shortage of jobs paying between £10,000 and £15,000pa, even in London. Many of these jobs are part-time but if £10.00 per hour becomes the minimum wage for a full time job (as has been suggested recently) multiply that by 40 hours a week, then by 52 weeks a year it comes to £20,800 a year - and that's before tax and NI deductions.

So its fair to suggest that the real average wage or salary is closer to £15,000 per year, of which about £10,000 will be take home pay. That's just over £192 a week, and you aren't buying a home for that.

You aren't able to afford current rents on it either.

Which is why that army I mentioned at the start of this chapter already exists. It's not a big army yet - but it will be.

13 War, Peace and Terror

I know not with what weapons World War III will be fought, but World War IV will be fought with sticks and stones

Albert Einstein (1879-1955)

Even as these words were being first written, US President Trump ordered fifty missiles to be fired at a Syrian Air base in retaliation for the country's President Assad using chemical weapons in an attack on a rebel town in Syria's then six-year old civil war.

President Trump subsequently declared that North Korea must give up its nuclear weapons and behave itself or the USA would deal with that country as well.

Somebody had obviously rattled his cage as during his election campaign, Trump consistently said that the US should stop involving itself in armed conflicts around the world. So his sabre was also being rattled, as was that of his opposite number, North Korean President Kim Jong-Un.

Was this any of our business? Is it now? Well, it might be. The problem with sitting on one side of the world and looking askance at something happening on the other side is that things have a nasty habit of spreading their way across the oceans and to our doorstep. Sometimes the rate of progress from there to here can be mind-bendingly rapid, as history tells us - if that is, we care to remember it and learn from it. One thing we have become very good at in the UK is not doing so. Yet it is only by remembering the events of the past that we can avoid repeating the same mistakes, either in the present or the future - and we don't.

Who today knows how World War I started? It's a fair bet that there are quite a number who don't have the slightest idea, including many current politicians. A reminder; WWI did not start because of our wicked imperialist, capitalist system and it was not the result of a class struggle either. It began because somebody assassinated somebody else (an Archduke called Ferdinand) in a place nobody had ever heard of at the time called Sarajevo, and his guys got their mates, who were bigger than the first somebody involved. The first somebody then got *their* mates, who were bigger still and suddenly thousands were dying in muddy fields across France and Belgium. That may well be a very simple version but its still the rub of it.

Sarajevo is the capital of Bosnia-Herzegovina so it has cropped up again a few times since then. But its still a long way from London, just as London is an even greater distance from Pyongyang (North

Korea's capital). So just because something is going on a long way away, it doesn't mean that the UK won't be dragged into it for one reason or another.

World War II was a slightly different ball game in that we went into it despite then Prime Minister Neville Chamberlain hopping across the channel for a chat with Nazi Germany's leader Adolf Hitler and getting what Chamberlain thought was a great deal. Chamberlain is probably best known for that oft-repeated newsreel clip of him on the steps of the aircraft that brought him back from Germany, waving his piece of paper (the agreement that he and Hitler had come to) and declaring peace in our time. Hitler's forces had been storming across Europe sweeping all before them as the Nazis wanted what Hitler described as *'Lebensraum'* or 'living space' for the German people. Since the UK had a defence agreement with our east European ally Poland, when Germany invaded that country, Neville Chamberlain declared war on Germany - and so it began all over again, only twenty-one years after the last one.

Hitler may have conquered Europe but he didn't conquer the UK. This country hasn't been invaded since 1066 (and for those who don't know about 1066, go and look it up). The nearest Nazi Germany came to it was occupying the Channel Islands. Britain led the fightback against Nazi aggression with that well-known aerial event called the Battle of Britain, the Royal Air Force and its pilots going down in history as 'The Few'.

Fast forward to David Cameron's time as Prime Minister and my earlier comments about today's politicians not knowing much about anything was graphically illustrated by his crass remark about the UK being 'The junior partner' in the Second World War, a remark that he was rightly derided for.

The UK's involvement with Afghanistan is another example of the lessons of history not being learnt; there are countless examples of foreign forces trying to occupy the country and failing - the USSR was the most recent prior to the western-led attempt. Iraq was and remains another. There may or may not have been justification for the invasions of both, depending in your point of view but the real reasons for them were the same reasons that Tony Blair was so keen to involve the UK in various armed conflicts around the world, and the same reasons yet again for David Cameron's desire for the UK to get involved in Libya and Syria - and yet once more, former US President George W. Bush had the same reasons for wanting to invade Afghanistan.

In 1982, Margaret Thatcher was still in her first term as Prime Minister. She was struggling to bring the UK back from the industrial anarchy of the 1970s under both Labour and Thatcher's predecessor as Tory leader, Edward Heath. It had been a remorselessly strike-ridden decade in which union militancy and left-wing dogma had the upper hand. All that culminated in what became known as the Winter of Discontent, when rubbish piled up in the streets as waste went uncollected. The dead remained unburied. A time conveniently ignored and forgotten about today, but a time that led to Thatcher's Conservatives winning the 1979 General Election comfortably. The country had had enough of pointless and unnecessary strikes - but that first term of office was extraordinarily difficult. After three years, questions were asked about the wisdom of Thatcher, rumours of a possible leadership challenge had begun to bubble a little; only a little but they were there.

Margaret Thatcher's great fortune was the invasion by Argentina of the Falkland Islands in 1982. Few people in the UK had ever heard of the islands, never mind knowing where they were. The where was not too far from the coast of Argentina, just off the tip of its southernmost point, in the (very) South Atlantic Ocean and some 8,000 miles from the UK. Despite the distance its people were steadfastly British. Argentina call the islands *'Las Islas Malvinas'* and their claim to them is also a long-standing one. The dispute between the two countries had lasted for decades but a military conflict had never arisen. Both countries got along reasonably well, despite the occasional diplomatic hiccup over the islands, and trade links were quite good. So why did Argentina choose to take the islands by force? The answer to that lies in yet another failing dictatorship, that of General Leopoldo Galtieri. Like all dictatorships, Galtieri's wasn't terribly good and the country's economy was in even worse shape that the UK. One thing South Americans tend not to be is quiet and submissive; they can be very vocal in protesting and Argentina's people were justifiably restless. Faced with the collapse of domestic order Galtieri needed something to restore his popularity. So he and his military junta ordered the invasion, reasoning that the islands were too far away for the UK to respond to it, was cutting its defence expenditure massively and had too many other things to worry over anyway. Argentina's un-elected dictator was wrong.

The Falklands conflict is one of the defining moments of modern British history and the successful mission to retake the islands one of the UK's military triumphs. It also defined Margaret Thatcher's premiership. She became known as a Prime Minster not to be trifled with, leading a country not to be trifled with. Suddenly, the United Kingdom began to walk tall again. It had demonstrated that it was not a country to be bullied or intimated. Thatcher went on to serve as Prime Minister for another eight years, being succeeded by John Major. Major's time however was the opposite of Thatcher, even though he won the General Election of 1992. His government was replaced by that of Tony Blair in 1997 and as well as his other ambitions mentioned earlier, Blair wanted his Thatcher moment, his

Falklands. As did George W. Bush and so did David Cameron. While Bush had justification for doing something after the attacks on the USA in September 2001, both Blair and Cameron wanted to stride the world stage, to be seen and acknowledged as great World Statesmen. Both failed. Despite their eagerness to show themselves as hard men, as Leaders with whom you did not mess, neither came close to achieving the status of leadership they wanted - and both, Cameron especially, had ruthlessly cut defence spending.

What of the lessons of history? Under David Cameron, although he maintained that the Falklands would remain British (as did Blair) one of the issues over mounting a military assault was whether or not the country could actually do it. Before Margaret Thatcher's election as Prime Minister, Labour (under Jim Callaghan) had already initiated severe cuts to defence, including the impending withdrawal of the Royal Navy's aircraft carriers. Thatcher's government had continued to do so, despite repeated warnings from the Services that the UK would have no 'unforeseen event response' capability if the cuts continued. The Falklands conflict gave some respite to cutting defence but once Tony Blair's New Labour had assumed power, the cuts resumed and were even more significant under David Cameron. It has long been a point of commentators that were Argentina to mount a second invasion today, the UK simply does not have the means to repeat the feats of 1982.

Defence cutbacks have been a fact of life since the end of WWII. In 1945 and the years immediately following, it is probably fair to say that Her Majesty's Armed Forces were bigger than at any time before or since. A visible services presence was required for a variety of reasons in a number of places around the world and at home, a specific threat was perceived from a visible potential enemy – what was the USSR. Those circumstances however no longer apply. There is an inevitability that the physical size of HM Forces will be considerably lower today than it once was. Which does not mean that the UK no longer faces any kind of threat. It does.

We need to decide exactly what the purpose of having a Navy, an Army and an Air Force actually is. Few would disagree with the premise that the primary purpose is to defend the UK and its citizens from attack and to deter any potential aggressor from so doing and most would agree that they do not exist to pander to the desires of Prime Ministers who wish to swagger around the globe and show how tough they are, as has been the case with both Tony Blair and David Cameron.

However, do we actually have enough to deter anybody from attacking us? Is there any enemy of the UK that, either overtly or covertly, threatens the country with military attack? Possibly.

North Korea may be one, although that only because of its long-standing enmity towards the USA and its desire to reclaim the South of the country as its own. It is deterred from trying because of the USA's heavy involvement with South Korea.

Interestingly (and again since the first edition of this book was published) US President Trump's aggressive stance towards North Korea and the trading of insults between him and Kim Jong Un appears to have paid dividends. Trump, like Bush, Blair and Cameron, wants to be seen as a great leader, somebody who stands up for his country. The verbal fisticuffs actually brought the two Presidents together for a meeting in Singapore and, for now at least, something of an accord appears to have been reached. Whether it ultimately results in peace on the Korean peninsula remains to be seen but President Trump seems to have had his own Thatcher moment. Of a sort, at least.

What about Russia? The country's President, Vladimir Putin, may be many things but what he is not is unintelligent. He is a smart man and knows fine well that Russia's economy depends on being able to trade with the rest of the world, particularly in terms of energy. So even allowing for the occasional bout of bellicosity, a military conflict is improbable. Not impossible though and more likely over an incident involving Russian and Western forces in an unstable area like Syria.

China? Even less likely than Russia. China has long been seen as having a threat potential greater than anybody but again, how many people realise that many of the common brand name products we buy are made in China? Trade disputes will come and go but China's well-being depends on its ability to sell things to the rest of the world.

Globalisation has its critics but in a world where so many countries are now inter-dependent on each other, and those countries' prosperity (along with that of their leaders) has become so definitively linked, only a fool or the strikingly dim would take the risk

How about Iran? One should never say never. But how many potential aggressors are there? In truth, the answer is impossible to define. Whilst one country may be readily identified as a threat, again history tells us that sometimes the threat comes from an entirely unexpected source – precisely the point made by the British Services Chiefs-Of-Staff prior to the Falklands conflict (and since).

If one cannot actually specify a threat or the potential of one, it could be said that there is little point in having any armed services at all. Yet all the World's nations, without exception, face the same threat today; that of militant, heavily-armed, organised and efficient terrorism, mostly backed by religious zealotry.

The problem with terrorism is one that is easily recognized; you can't recognize it. The terrorist does not wear a uniform and does not play by any rules of engagement. The terrorist does not stand fast on the field of battle and engage you directly. This we all know. The biggest Army, the biggest Navy, the biggest Air Force is of little use against the fanatic armed only with a van in a busy street, or a hidden bomb in a crowded shopping mall. We know that too.

So how do you stop a terrorist? How do you stop an unhinged individual who is willing to take their own life in order to kill as many people as possible completely at random as they go about their normal day-to-day business?

You can't.

That may be hard to take, but what is the aim of the terrorist? His aim is simple; to force us to give up our way of life and bend ourselves to his. The terrorist is the dictator by another name and another method - and every time another new law is created, another restriction is put in place, and by our Government, the terrorist wins. He wins because it is our freedom that is taken away in the name of protecting us.

We have the right to go about doing what we want to do without getting blown up, but to eliminate that risk means eliminating freedom. It is a price we should think very carefully about before paying. We still however, need our Armed Services and we need them to be of substantial size and substantially well-equipped, well-trained, up to date with the latest technology and armed to equal terms with what others in the world have. Whatever those arms may be.

Not to fight the expected, but to fight the unexpected.

■

14 The Price of Success

Facts do not cease to exist because they are ignored
Aldous Huxley (1894-1963)

Everyone knows (or should know) that there is a price to be paid for failure. The most well-known football managers, people who have won everything there is to win, have all been sacked at some point because they were perceived to be failures and the team they were managing didn't win a trophy or lost a few games. Once sacked, they are then re-employed by another club which has just sacked its own trophy-winning manager. Then they win something and get sacked again.

The merry-go-round that is football management and the sometimes slightly weird behaviour of those who do the hiring and firing, would probably make a book in its own right – Dutchman Louis Van Gaal won the FA Cup in his second season and was promptly sacked by Manchester United. Who says lightning doesn't strike twice - guess what? Back in the 1970s, Tommy Docherty won the FA Cup as manager of Manchester United and almost immediately got the push as well, so the bring-'em-in-then-boot-'em-out principle is not new (although the reason for Docherty's sacking was a little different; he had a affair with the wife of the club's physiotherapist). What would make life interesting is if the same standard of expectation was applied to every other industry that appoints managers (especially the NHS...). So while most people will accept, at least up to a point, that there is a price for failure, did you know there is a price for success as well?

Never really thought about it? Didn't think so. Well, there is - and paying for success can carry a bigger price to pay than the one for failing.

Tiger Woods was hailed as one of the world's best golfers and took the globe by storm when he first emerged but as his career went on, he became dogged by controversy over his personal life, the same applying to many other sportsmen and women. Those of a pitiless disposition (along with the unknowing) often smile and make various critical remarks but none stop and think about the way in which the most successful often have to sacrifice almost everything to *be* successful.

The same argument applies to most things; the more successful you are, the harder one has to work to remain so and the higher the price can be. Not everyone handles the expectation badly; there are numerous examples of successful people – whatever their chosen path – who manage to remain reasonably well-balanced and do not succumb to the pressure. The unknowing also cast some doubt on what pressure actually means; some will say that pressure is wondering if one has enough food to eat each week and that the successful don't have to worry about money. That may well be true but once one is a success, one is also expected to stay a success. The criticisms levelled at people who are thought to be good at something can become so great that the personality buckles and the flaws present in all of us then come to the fore, hence the fall from grace of Tiger Woods. He is not alone.

Book authors, having produced a good book that everybody buys and reads then has to do it again - and then again. Footballers, having scored the great goal, have to score again and again. The factory assembly worker, having assembled greatly, has to continue to do so, day after day after day. There are times, and many of them, when the pressure we find ourselves under, can be too much. So even though most people want to be good at something, when we are and we succeed, we need to understand that while we get the price of failure, we also have to pay the price of success. Success can be as destructive as any illness and sometimes even more so than failure.

22 May 2017: A mentally defective individual blew himself up in the foyer of a concert hall in Manchester, killing twenty-two people, ten of them teenage girls and one an eight-year-old girl. Hundreds more were injured.

In the days following, pages and pages of newsprint were expended on terror attacks and so on. Social media was full of instantaneous knee-jerk vitriol. Most commentary was more moderate in reaction, but a significant number (to the shame of those who posted them) were along the lines of 'round up all Muslims and kick 'em out, and stuff their human rights'.

On the Wednesday after the bombing, the Daily Mail and like all newspapers, having carried those pages of coverage, said the following in the leader column on page 20:

> 'The fact is that more than 3,000 jihadis are based in the UK...yet thanks to the wretched Nick Clegg's hand-wringing over civil liberties, a mere seven are subject to terrorism prevention orders.
>
> How many more atrocities must we suffer before we routinely tag suspects and stop putting their human rights above our own safety?'

The Price of Success

Columnist Sarah Vine (Conservative MP Michael Gove's wife) ended her full-page article, the main thrust of which was of the young girls murdered and the freedom we enjoy in western society, on page 21 with this:

> '...All had a lifetime of possibilities ahead of them. All were free. And for that they paid a terrible price.'

On page 19 of the same edition, John R. Bradley (mentioned earlier), an author of four books on the Middle East, in a three-column article, had this to say:

> '...However, we have a sex offenders register that for the most part does the job that it was designed to do, which is to monitor the activities and locations of those the state wants to keep tabs on.
>
> Why should we not go one step further and electronically tag Islamist terror suspects so we always know where they are? They should also, like sex offenders, be banned from using the internet.'

There is the problem, right there. Do forgive the repetition (again) but if justice is to be really just, if freedom is to *mean* freedom, then you cannot ban people from the internet, the main tool for communication today; to do anything, one must 'go online' and use the internet - and that includes getting advice from the government itself. In the extract above, John R. Bradley says, 'to monitor the activities and locations of those the state wants to keep tabs on. Why should we not go one step further...'

The idea of the state keeping tabs on anybody it wants to should be a worrying prospect. As I have said already, if we really are a free society, then you cannot electronically tag or restrict people in case they 'might' do something and even less so as a matter of 'routine' as the Mail suggested. Justice cannot be pro-active. It can only be reactive. Somebody has to 'do' something before punishment is doled out.

So yes Miss Vine freedom does have a price and yes it is high and yes, it can be terribly so.

And Mr. Bradley, it is always 'one step further' to ultimate oppression and that way lies only the complete subjugation of a free people.

We are, in essence, a successful society, despite the irrefutably huge flaws we have. If terrorists are to be defeated, we pay the price of success and freedom and take the risks of success and freedom.

Otherwise we are not free. And we will not be successful.

▪

15 For Sale; One country, formerly known as the UK
(Infrastructure included; note – large profits to be made out of a compliant and subservient population)

The train now arriving on platform one is on fire. Passengers are advised not to board this train.

Station Announcer, Bournemouth

On Facebook recently –

Don M -	Do you know we had a motor industry before we joined the common market?
Kevan James -	Didn't they spend a lot of time on strike?
Barrie L -	Didn't they sell dinky toys?
Don M -	It was a mess but it could have been sorted.
John A -	Plus fishing and steel and our own laws.
Michael R -	We also owned our own infrastructure, telecoms, water, railways, council house's etc. etc…nothing to do with Europe - just a badly run country.
Barrie L -	This country is run by the rich for the rich.
Jeff G -	And you plebs had better not forget it. Now go and get that ten acres poised...
David W -	"Poised"??
Jeff G	Yeah, it's Somerset for plowed. (Look, I have no idea how or why this bloody tablet changes what I write….ok?)

Government Notice (posted at ports, airports and in Global Financial publications)

> For sale - The UK, along with its essential infrastructure, including rail, air and sea terminals. Electricity, Gas and all other energy sources are also available. Particularly welcome are bids for housing.
> We are pleased to offer all the above (and more, especially Football Clubs) for immediate acquisition.
> We have subdued the population and they will meekly accept your hikes in the cost of everything to them.
> As we no longer make anything in the UK, new owners are welcome to close what remains of out factories and shift production elsewhere so big profits are guaranteed.
> Buy now!

Speculation abounds that (if it actually does get built) the new HS2 high speed rail line linking London with a little of the north-west and centre of England may be operated by the Chinese. It seems that one of the global companies wanting to make an offer to operate the service is a consortium of the Hong Kong firm MTR and the Guangshen Railway Company (China already has a big stake in the Hinkley Point Nuclear power plant as well as in increasing involvement in other areas of UK life). Right before this book went to print, railway ticket machines across the country shut down due to an 'IT glitch' A German firm, Scheidt & Bachmann, supplies the software and systems for the machines. Cadbury, that ancient and long-established firm of chocolate makers is today owned by US giant Kraft. The Japanese own the biggest manufacturers of cars in the UK, Nissan in Sunderland and Toyota near Derby. Also in Derby, the very epicentre of railway construction at one time, what remains of the rail manufacturing industry there is owned by Bombardier, who are Canadian. Heathrow Airport is owned by a Spanish-led consortium. Our energy suppliers, gas and electricity, are owned by foreign companies. English Football is owned by foreigners, managed and coached by foreigners and played by foreigners. The list is, now, almost endless.

As a slight aside, some of the biggest owners of British businesses are not based within the EU; the trade rules emanating from Brussels has not stopped the rest of the world beating a path to the UK door to buy everything. The latest, and yet again since the first edition of this book was published, was GKN - a company that has been supplying the British military with various things since the days of cannon balls is now owned by foreign interests.

How did we get here? Why is it that the UK no longer makes anything, provides anything or owns anything? Those of a certain political persuasion will tell you that it is all the fault of Thatcher, and started when she sold everything in the 1980s. Whilst it is true that the Thatcher government engaged in mass privatisation during its term of office, not all of it was during her leadership. The sale of Britain's railway companies and the tracks the trains run on was done by John Major's government, but it is not only the Conservatives that have sold off UK assets; The Royal Mail was privatised under Labour.

So why was it done? In the 1980s, when it all started, Thatcher's government knew that Britain's infrastructure needed serious money putting into it. Everything was getting old, from the systems that supply our water and treat the waste we produce, to energy, everything. Successive Governments, both Tory *and* Labour, had signally failed to keep everything working properly, the result being that the UK did not have the money to renew it and bring it up to date - billions were needed. The privatisation idea was sold to the British public on the basis that it would lead to more consumer choice as companies would have to compete with each other to keep our custom, but this was a little misleading; the real reason was that the UK couldn't afford to pay the price of bringing everything up to date.

A privately owned company works in one of two ways; either you are seriously rich and own a company outright. If you do, than you are responsible for it. Do it right, it makes a profit. If it makes a profit it stays in business and people have jobs. Most companies have to keep themselves up-to-date with everything, including new ways of doing business, new technology, new equipment to replace that which wears out or becomes obsolete, and so on. Doing that costs money; if your company makes seriously good money and earns more than it spends, then the cash needed to keep up-to-date can come from those earnings, along with the tax your company has to pay, and whatever it costs to actually run the company (wages, energy bills and so on). This is otherwise known as a 'surplus of income over expenditure' and whatever is left after you have paid for everything is the actual profit. However, even if you do personally own the company, that profit isn't yours – it belongs to the company so you can't just stick in your back pocket. It has to go in to the company's bank account. What you do after that of course, is up to you, it is your company and you can do what you like, at least up to a point. But if you want to get some outside help, for example, to buy new equipment, that usually comes from a bank loan. Banks aren't going to lend you a penny if your company doesn't have a healthy profit because you spend it on another house in Marbella. So the profit goes in to the company bank account. If you decide you want to sell up, your buyer is also going to want to see what kind of profit the company makes as well. On top of that, there are some legal aspects involved, one of which is that if things go sour, you personally are responsible for everything so you are liable.

An alternative is to have a Board of Directors. Directors usually become Directors by investing their own money, thus giving them the right to have a say in what goes on but the company is still owned by the Directors, as opposed a single individual. Having a Board of Directors also usually means becoming a Limited Liability Company, which acted as a safeguard for the Directors if things went badly and the company closed down. That's changed a little over recent times so that Directors can no longer simply walk away with no personal loss if a company went bust.

The second way is to open the company up to outside interests and have shareholders. Shareholders become so by buying shares, thus raising extra money for the company to use (like replacing older equipment and expanding the business). In return for buying shares, shareholders can expect to be paid an annual dividend, so they make something out of it. Boards of Directors are thus responsible to the company's shareholders.

This is something that most people don't quite grasp. When something is perceived to be wrong, a service doesn't work the way you think it should (or indeed, doesn't work) people moan about customer service and make demands like 'sack the board'. But the Board are not responsible to you, even if you are a customer. The Board's first responsibility is to the company shareholders - nobody else. Having said that, it follows that the better run a company is, the more satisfied customers will be, so the bigger the profits, the happier shareholders will be and everything is rosy.

When privatisation took hold, one of the selling points to those who opposed it was that a minimum number of shares had to be made available to the British public and British investors and kept by those who bought them for a set minimum period of time. As that time expired, the problem has been that, over the years, British shareholding has been diluted by those shareholdings being sold, either directly or by the sale of the business itself; if you own a share or two, after that period of time, there was nothing to stop you making a profit by selling them to whoever makes you the best offer – you paid £2.50 per share and ten years later, somebody offers you £5 per share (or more), few people refused; the business is doing very well, so the value of your shares go up (the opposite can also happen by the way, and does). In the same way, because the business is doing well, the Board of Directors, who are also shareholders, receive an offer which they then recommend to other shareholders. The company is then sold and everybody walks away with a tidy profit. The problem was that British expertise was in high demand. Formerly state-owned businesses were doing well and good businesses are always attractive acquisitions, so the world beat a path to the UK's doors to buy any good business - and since the buying and selling of shares is done on the open market, and is thus open to anybody, anybody can make an offer to buy shares. No matter where they come from.

There is admittedly, a little more to it, but put simply, the result is that much of the UK is now owned by foreign interests. Very big global corporations have very big cash reserves and there are few companies based solely within one country that have the same financial strength so saying 'no' to an attractive offer is often very difficult.

The only problem is that, the bigger a company gets, the more successful it becomes, the less approachable it becomes as well. The size of its profits means that if you don't like it and take your custom elsewhere, the company that loses your business can shrug and say, *'So what? We have plenty of other customers'* and that customer base is spread around the world, rather than in just one country. Given that so much of the world is, as I have already said, now inter-dependent on everywhere else, whether one likes it or not, foreign ownership is here to stay.

It has some advantages and some disadvantages. One of the drawbacks is that the use of language has become standardised and has so as a result of needing to make everything easily understood by everybody, regardless of where in the world they are. The result of that is that there are phrases and words in use now that weren't before and this is something that many ordinary people find less desirable:

Facebook on Corporate-speak

Fay J -	Corporate-speak is absolutely hideous. We're not people but 'resources': "Can you allocate a resource to do this" instead of "Can you get someone to do this"
John B -	'Skill set' pisses me off, too.
Ramon K -	And all the 'new terms' which are basically known for ages but not trendy enough
Jens N -	'Solution Architect' is great as well.
Gary **W** -	'Run it up the flagpole, see who salutes' is one I heard.

Comments of a Common Man

Derek S -	'All singing from the same Hymn sheet '.
George M -	'Outside the box' and 'the bigger picture'...all crap to me.
Cliff F -	'Let's touch base', 'at the end of the day'. they all do my head in....it's all bollox
Cliff F -	Oh and how could I forgot the best one of them all.....when someone is being interviewed on TV, the person replying starts off by saying "So" to every question...
Alex K -	'This vehicle is fitted with recording technology'... (you mean its fitted with a video camera).
Alex K -	'Your a member of a well valued team of colleagues'... (you mean you work with other people doing same job).
Gary W -	Don't forget the old classic, 'there is no I in team'... but there is a U in f**k up though.
Ron B -	So. You're quite the cranky resource this morning.....
Kevan James -	All hail to plain speaking - it will be covered in my new book 'Comments of a Common Man'. This volume of textual information is accessible for immediate acquisition.

Do you want to be a resource or a real person?

There has been something of a move towards plain English but as the above reveals, use (or misuse) of language has become rather common. Supermarkets today do not have staff. They have 'colleagues'. Signs abound saying that if you want help, ask a colleague. *But I don't work here! These folks, as helpful as they are, are not my colleagues!*

Perhaps next time I go into my local ASDA, Morrisons or Tesco, I should send them an invoice for the time I spent there since the staff are, apparently, my colleagues.

Now, there's a thought….maybe if everybody did that, those who work there, and as helpful as they always are, might become members of staff once again.

Having mentioned ASDA, it might be worth pointing out that they are another company now owned by a foreign concern, in this case, Wal-Mart of the USA (at least until they sell it or merge it with Sainsbury). Like all the others, without exception, they have an irritating habit. Two actually; the first is every so often, they move things around their stores. Just as one has got used to finding things, they suddenly appear on the other side of the store. Why do they do it? To keep customers on their toes? To make us exercise more as we trail around trying to find something? Actually it's done to make us – the customer – spend more time wandering and as we do so, we might spot something we hadn't thought of and buy it. In other words, manipulating our time in the store to increase our possible purchases. Another little trick concerns those goods that we buy the most of and usually the cheapest. Something sells well. Enough people buy it for it to run out regularly. The obvious answer would be to stock less of the things that aren't selling well and more of the things that do. Not a chance! Such a customer-friendly idea is anathema! What happens is that the best-selling product disappears from the shelves entirely and thus you are forced into paying more for an alternative - which is why your weekly shopping bill keeps going up. You will pay the price…

And going back to the subject of being successful at something (and paying the price for it), some female, aged seventeen, bought a Euromillions lottery ticket a while ago and won a million pounds. Having spent most of it, she later went public, got airtime on TV and her name and face in national newspapers by threatening to sue lottery operator Camelot because winning made her miserable and says she should not have bought a ticket at seventeen because seventeen is too young to handle such a win. Apparently she wanted compensation amounting to one million pounds…

This was also reinforced at the beginning of August 2018, by *another* young lady who won £1.87 million at the age of sixteen in 2003. Now aged thirty-one (and like the other, appearing on TV) she too says sixteen is too young to buy a lottery ticket.

Both blew all their winnings on boob jobs and similar fripperies, with one admitting spending £250,000 on cocaine.

Both these young ladies say that sixteen and seventeen is 'far too young' to buy tickets and thus win large amounts of money on the lottery. The older of the two also said, 'At sixteen you are still just a child and overnight you've got to grow up and become an adult, which is very difficult'.

Welcome to the world – the real world – of growing older. Whether you like it or not.

Yet they (along with other sixteen and seventeen-year-olds) want the right to vote? Yeah right... I bet they still want the right to have sex at sixteen and seventeen too. Actually it's the government who decides on the minimum age, not Camelot. If you are too young to buy a lottery ticket at sixteen and seventeen, you are too young to vote and you are too young to have sex – wait until you are eighteen.

Even at eighteen growing up still has some distance to cover – what price age then? Is growing older really such a bad thing (*Logan's Run*...)? Or are they merely money-grabbing chancers on the make?

Look, it's very simple. Cut the crap and just give me a few millions. I'm happy to pay the price of having lots of money, it won't make me miserable, I don't want Camelot's army of advisers telling me what to do and I'll give the money a loving home.

I promise.

16 Plebiscite

A party manifesto should be a Lighthouse not a Shop Window

Winston Churchill

2017.

In yet another example of the fast-moving world of politics and again right on the cusp of the first edition of this book going to print, the Prime Minister, Theresa May, called a General Election, held on 8 June.

The Political parties released their Manifestos, their list of promises, things they will do if elected. Nobody actually believes the manifestos, even the parties themselves probably don't believe them and every election campaign is peppered with promises that are actually not in the manifestos - and every time a leading party member says one thing, the other parties seize upon it and promise the opposite. Interestingly, manifestos are not legally binding documents; as loath as I am to suggest the introduction of new laws perhaps it is time they were. If political parties were obliged by law not only to carry out those promises, but also to be specific in how they would be financed (since they are asking us, the people, to employ them to run our country for us *and* pay for it...) then said parties might be less inclined to be so flamboyant in what they say they will do if elected

The Conservatives have always been perceived as the party of low taxation, Labour of high taxation; various high-ups in the Tory party as the 2017 campaign got underway, demanded that Theresa May state unequivocally that they would lower taxes. May herself said 'They would keep taxes as low as possible.' Labour immediately promised to 'slash VAT'.

Who to believe?

What *is* easily believed is the speed with which career politicians and their advisors leap upon anything perceived to be popular or 'right'. With the suicide bombing in Manchester, election campaigning was suspended. When a second incident happened in London the weekend before the election date, campaigning was again suspended. Yet those same politicians consistently stated that our way of life must not change and we should go about doing the things we always do.

So why were there two incidents after the election had been called and one just four days before the day itself? To stop us doing the things we always do; to disrupt ordinary lives; to cause mayhem at a time most calculated to bring freedom to a halt. By suspending the election campaign, 'right-on' politicians play into the hands of the opponents of freedom. Rather perversely the attacks did at least give the ordinary person a little relief from the interminable droning of those politicians all contradicting each other and making wild promises about things they cannot possibly control if elected and simply hurling pointless insults at each other.

The so-called Leaders Debates – I watched these, out of novelty value as much as anything when they were first aired. I expected little and got even less. Gordon agreeing with Nick on almost everything was cringeworthy at the time and the memory doesn't make it less so. I wasn't terribly impressed with David Cameron either but there is little doubt that Nick Clegg performed quite well. Unfortunately, that's just what it was; a performance, as his time (along with others from the Liberal Democrats) in a coalition proved. The problem with the Liberal Democrats is that they have been a minority party for so long they have become little more than a protest group, one that can oppose everything, say anything yet never have the responsibility of running something.

These debates become even more pointless when they include parties that do not have nationwide candidates and do not aspire to govern the United Kingdom, a point which applies to the Scottish Nationalists more than any other. Why was Nicola Sturgeon invited? She isn't even a serving MP. She may well be present in the Scottish Parliament but she is not in the United Kingdom Parliament. Until or unless she is, and does so seeking to govern the UK, she has little nationwide credibility and no place in a National TV debate pertaining to a UK General Election.

Why are we having these debates? They are an imported Americanism and have no real part to play in this country. They work quite well in the USA but there is one important difference; when it comes to election time itself, there are only two participants, both of whom want to be President of the United States. For the most part, those two candidates are worth listening to (although not always). The string of people lassoing the audience in these debates in the UK borders on the ridiculous, gives little time for each of them to make a serious point and results in each of them shouting over the others. Since most of them have no chance whatsoever in becoming Prime Minister, what was the point of them being there? At least the Brown/Cameron/Clegg debates involved the three party leaders who stood a chance of becoming the Prime Minister of the country.

So what of this time around, in 2017? The most notable was the BBC debate in which Theresa May sent then Home Secretary Amber Rudd instead of taking part herself. A perfect example of those hiding behind Jeremy Corbyn's Labour party was the behaviour of the audience; every time Corbyn said anything, the whoops and hoots were at best, unedifying, at worst hooliganistic and even more so in the treatment meted out to Amber Rudd. The former Home Secretary is not my favourite politician but she did remarkably well in the face of outright hostility and bias. One can't really blame Theresa May for not taking part.

It is also the perfect example of why such TV 'debates' have no place in the UK, during election campaigns or at any other time.

□

Jeremy Corbyn has been consistent over decades in his beliefs. He is an avowed far-left socialist and well-known for being so. He has always, since being elected as an MP, been something of a maverick, willing to buck the trend and go against the party line. Of itself that's not necessarily a bad thing but he also has two big flaws; firstly, like many others in Politics, he has never held a real job in the real world and secondly, he has also shown demonstrative support for organisations like the IRA, Hezbollah and HAMAS, organisations that set off bombs in crowded city centres, killing ordinary people.

He had also never held a front-line job in Government for Labour. So how did he get to be leader of the party?

The answer is that it was rigged – twice – in his favour. By opening up membership of the party to everybody and anybody (again of itself not a bad thing but only of itself) and charging a nominal and extraordinarily low membership fee, the floodgates were opened to the extreme left, those that had been purged from the party during its wild excesses of the 1970s and 1980s. These were people who hid behind the cloak of respectability, the name of the Labour Party and their actions all those years ago proved their opposition to freedom and democracy.

They never went away however. They never vanished into cyberspace like a deleted file - and most significantly, they never formed their own political party and campaigned honestly for what they wanted to do. They didn't simply because they know fine well that they would never be elected to govern the UK. They needed, still need, to hide behind something more acceptable, and the Labour Party, with the inherent flaws within it described earlier in this book, provides the perfect cover.

So an absurdly low membership fee and an open to all-comers policy allowed them back in and the lure was the ability, as party members, to vote for its leader. The upsurge in Labour Party membership was due to the return of so many extremists, hence Corbyn's election as leader.

Now look at what happened when a capable MP like Angela Eagle wanted to stand against Corbyn; threats against her forced her to withdraw, and she was not the only one. A number of Labour MPs were on the end of the same and all from those hiding behind

Jeremy Corbyn. Not only that but since Corbyn became leader, there has been a disturbing rise in Anti-Semitism, including towards those Labour MPs who happen to be Jewish. Corbyn has spoken against it but has he spoken strongly enough? There are increasing numbers who say not, including Jewish newspapers in the UK and, more significantly perhaps, long-standing members of the Labour party itself. Is Jeremy Corbyn an Anti-Semite? My own guess is no, he is not, but that said, he does have past associations with, and has spoken in support of, organisations whose aim is the destruction of Israel. Whether Corbyn is or is not Anti-Semitic, it remains the case that extremism has grown within the Labour party in recent times.

It is the biggest single issue with the far left. It has a tendency to attract those who are utterly intolerant of anybody who does not agree with everything it stands for and has been proved to be so throughout history – most or even all of the most oppressive dictatorships have been the result of the far left gaining power.

As long as those elements are present within Labour, the party cannot be trusted with freedom and democracy.

The Tories also have their faults and many of them. Theresa May is, just like Jeremy Corbyn, an essentially honest and dedicated politician. She has her quirks (again like Corbyn), one of the most well-known for being something of a fashionista, with a taste for sometimes eye-catching footwear. She was also the one of the longest serving Home Secretaries and managed to achieve something her predecessors didn't, namely the deportation of several religious hate preachers, who consistently called upon those of like mind to kill people.

May also has the distinction of being one of only two women Prime Ministers the UK has ever had; despite its demonstrable commitment to gender equality, Labour has never had a woman leader or Prime Minister; the Conservatives have, the other of course, was Margaret Thatcher.

There may be some reading this who know not of how it all works. My bet is that most readers probably will know (otherwise you might not be reading) but for those that don't, there are two Houses of Parliament; the House of Lords (which we will leave alone for the purposes of this chapter) and the House of Commons. The Commons, often called simply 'the House', is the one that counts. So what does it actually do? It passes new laws, and…er….that's it really. It doesn't actually do much else. Occasionally it repeals old laws, and in theory, it is where the Government can be called to account for what it does. If you have a gripe about something, you can get in touch with your MP, who and again theoretically at least, can raise your gripe in the House by asking the Minster responsible to look into it. The most well-known occasion is every Wednesday during Prime Minister's Questions, when the PM has to answer questions tabled by MPs (your MP can raise gripes at any time however and not just in the House).

The Government is formed by whichever party has the most MPs elected. I'm not going to go into all the ancient history of it all (if you want to know that, look it up) but since 1945, only two parties have won elections outright; the Conservatives and Labour. That's been broken a couple of times by neither party having had enough MP's elected to have an outright majority of MPs in the House of Commons, known as a 'hung parliament', in 1974 and the most recent being 2010, when the Conservatives, under Cameron, had the most MPs but not quite enough so formed a coalition with the Liberal Democrats, the first time in living memory the Lib-Dems had actually been in Government.

2017 result - it's a hung parliament...or as some rather laughingly put it, a 'balanced' parliament...there is nothing 'balanced' about it. To run the country, the country needs a party with a majority in parliament to do it.

The country seems more divided than ever, not just politically but in age (young and old) and in the main voters returned to both the Conservatives and Labour, abandoning the smaller parties – Nick Clegg booted out. Alex Salmond and Angus Robertson out in Scotland (independence not wanted and the disappearance of Alex Salmond would have resulted in ribald remarks from a late colleague of my dad, Peter McDonagh, mentioned earlier in this book, who called him the Baboon of Brigadoon), Jo Swinson back for the Lib Dems in Scotland, Vince Cable back in Twickenham. Zac Goldsmith won back Richmond Park for the Tories having lost to the Liberal-Democrats in a bye-election over London's Heathrow Airport's expansion with a majority of just 45. That kind of narrow result was repeated all over the country, for example Kensington, one of the wealthiest constituencies in the country, returned a Labour MP, doing so for the first time in history, albeit with a majority of just 20. Julian Brazier lost a 10,000 majority in Canterbury (Tory since 1918!) to Labour who now have a majority of just 185, with a very strong youth voter turnout being cited as the reason.

Interestingly, some allegations were made a while after the election that the increased numbers of young people voting (and voting for Labour candidates) was because some were doing so twice; those at university – in places like Canterbury – voting in the places where they were studying *and* in their home towns. Whether true or not is a matter for speculation but no action seems to have been taken to get to the bottom of the allegations. Voting twice however, is illegal. The apparent swing towards Labour was also not entirely one-sided; Tory Ben Bradley won the Mansfield seat with 23,392 votes, which meant that Mansfield turned blue for the first time in that constituency's history. Acting returning officer Jacqueline Collins however – perhaps being so used to seeing a Labour winner in the constituency – mistakenly announced that Labour candidate and MP for the last three decades, Sir Alan Meale, had triumphed.

Whatever the swings and roundabouts, the result is that, from having a slender majority in Parliament, the Conservatives now don't have one at all. Yes, they have more MPs than the other parties and so are entitled to form a Government but getting their decisions through parliament has become much harder.

That majority; (and again for those who may not know), a party gets its Parliamentary majority if the number of MPs it has elected is more than the rest of all the other parties put together.

With 650 MPs in total, the figure needed for a majority is 326; get 326 MPs and no matter how the result is divided among the rest, you will have a majority. 650 minus your 326 leaves 324. You have a majority of one to get your decisions through parliament... The problems arise if somebody is ill when a vote in the House takes place, or your own MP's don't vote for the decision you want to make, or somebody steps down as an MP partway through your term of office; that can be because they die, get caught doing something wrong and have to resign (which has happened quite a lot in recent times) or otherwise can no longer serve. So a bye-election has to be held in that constituency...and if you lose...out of the window goes your majority. With your party now having 325 and all the other parties combined also having 325, clearly you have a problem running the country.

Although you need 326 MPs to reach a simple majority of the 650-seat House of Commons, in reality the number is actually smaller. The Speaker of the House of Commons (the one who sits in that high chair and shouts 'Order!' when things get a little rowdy) and his deputies are like everybody else, still serving MPs but do not vote since they are in charge of the House.

The interesting MPs are those of Northern Irish party, Sinn Féin; there are seven of them and they refuse to take their seats in the House as this means swearing an oath of loyalty to the Queen. Sinn Féin want to see a united Ireland so they will not take that oath. This means that the working majority needed is actually eleven fewer at 315. Provided of course, that you have your 326 to start with.

But the Conservatives no longer have 326 MPs...the result was:

Conservatives –	318,	down by 13.
Labour –	262,	up 30.
Scottish National Party–	35,	down by 21.
Liberal Democrats –	12,	up by 4.
Others –	13,	down by 2.

Plebiscite

Total - 640

Conservatives – 318, The rest of the parties combined – 322. So simply put, the Conservatives can be outvoted on everything. If, that is, the 322 choose to do so.

Those others include the ten MPs of the Democratic Unionist Party, also of Northern Ireland, and by forming an alliance with them, the Conservatives will then have a working majority of 328.

So since the figures above total 640, who are the missing ten? Sinn Féin and the Speaker and his deputies. What I said above about the Speaker and his deputies not voting is not quite true; in the event of a voting tie, they can then vote and convention says they must always support the Government. But even if the Speaker and his deputies could vote in the normal course of events, and did so in support of the Government, that's still only 321. Hence the need for support from another party, either in a coalition (as was the case with the 2010 election) or a looser arrangement whereby the Conservatives are supported by another party - like the DUP

The two parties have much in common; the full title of the Tories is the Conservative and Unionist Party, meaning that, among other things, they are committed to the union that makes up the UK. The same applies to the DUP (Unlike Sinn Féin and the Scottish Nationalists). Known as a 'Confidence and Supply' arrangement, the two parties did indeed combine their MPs, although Theresa May still cannot afford to lose any of them, either to bye-elections or those purportedly on her own side when it comes to getting the Government's policies through Parliament.

How did the Conservatives lose a majority and end up as the party with the most seats, yet no overall majority? Was it really necessary to call the election at all? The answer to that is no. Theresa May's party had a majority; not a big one but it would have been enough to get business done. So why do it? Why call the 2017 election?

Remember Gordon Brown? The Scotsman from Kirkcaldy who, as Chancellor under Tony Blair, kept the UK out of the Euro despite Blair's enthusiasm for it? That one act was probably Brown's single greatest as Chancellor given the economic problems of the single currency that the EU operates but one of the criticisms aimed at him was that having inherited leadership of the Labour party from Blair, and thus becoming Prime Minister, he had never won an election as party leader. Not long after he had become PM, Labour were doing quite well in the polls and there were calls for him to hold a General Election on the basis that he would give himself a full five year term as PM and be able to say that he had won an election in his own right. The trouble with doing that is that the polls could be wrong and you might lose…

So he bottled it. He took the easy path yet lost the 2010 election.

Not by much but he still lost. There was talk in 2010 that since David Cameron did not have a majority, Labour 'could' form a new Government and stay in power, but wiser heads in the party at the time said, *'Look, we don't have the most MPs, we didn't win so let's accept that and go into opposition'*. Hence David Cameron becoming Prime Minister in coalition with the Liberal Democrats, and Nick Clegg becoming Deputy PM.

Like Brown before her, Theresa May had inherited leadership and Premiership. Like Brown, her Government and the lady herself, was enjoying good poll ratings. Her critics say she called the election because she thought she would win and win handsomely. There may be some truth to that but its not actually an unreasonable premise. Why do anything you don't have to unless you think you will win? She should also be given some credit for doing what Brown did not have the courage to do and call an election.

Theresa May might well have felt like a right muffin after the election but she did at least have the guts to ask the country for its permission to keep her job. She might not have won outright but still managed to gain the biggest share of the total vote since Tony Blair at the height of his omnipotence - and she has fifty-six more MPs than Jeremy Corbyn's Labour. Given that one single aspect to it, the idea that Corbyn 'won' is patently absurd.

That's one big difference between 2017 and 2010; in 2010 those wise enough had accepted that Labour did not have the right to form a government. In 2017, with the mass influx into Labour of those extremists mentioned earlier, those same extremists that now keep Corbyn as leader, do not accept that they have no right to form a Government even with fifty-six fewer MPs. Whooping Corbyn supporters in the streets is indicative of the nature of some of those who lie behind him. *The Tories don't have a majority! Therefore WE are entitled to rule!*

Hold the presses! Right on the cusp of the first edition going to print, on BBC1's 'Question Time', (Thursday 22 June, 2017) the Tory MP David Lidington was continually shouted down by an audience member, whose earlier tirade had revealed him to be a supporter of Corbyn and he was proved to be so afterwards – the hard left's eternal viewpoint; nobody else is allowed.

Labour also gained thirty new MPs; that's actually not a bad showing. It still does not give Labour the right to form a government however. Not that the extremists care. All they are interested in is getting power and should they do so, they will keep it.

It may sound apocalyptic but if Corbyn's Labour do get to form a Government, they will go for the five-year maximum term and at the end of that, they will 'postpone' the next general election. Most likely they will cite 'security concerns' for doing so. But they will use any means necessary to remain in control and will do so until the UK's freedom – *your* freedom – is completely crushed.

You think not? See the above remark about Question Time. See the earlier comments about the threats made against Labour MPs who had spoken out against Corbyn; see Corbyn's acolyte, Shadow Chancellor John McDonnell, calling on Unions and others to hold mass demonstrations to 'bring down the Government'. Look at McDonnell's remark, 'Democracy doesn't work very well for us.'

Go back to earlier in this book and re-read the story of Cuthbert and his train journey. See dozens of examples of hard-left intimidation, from Trade Union extremism to virtually any area of life you care to name, to the old Soviet Union and more.

History tells us that it will be so.

So why did the Conservatives snatch near-defeat from the jaws of victory?

One answer is that they have proved themselves remarkably inept at getting their message across for going on for twenty-five years. Inept is probably an inadequate word…utterly incompetent might be more descriptive. That inability to connect was graphically shown in 2017 and at a time when Jeremy Corbyn was able to realise his own potential as a communicator with ordinary people. Theresa May has been criticised for not being approachable, for being wooden and not very televisual (whereas Corbyn is the opposite). That's because they are very different people. One's personality should not count against them and as for May's alleged unapproachability, I can testify otherwise - I have met her, twice, and both times found her easy to talk to and happy to do so. What did count against May was her reliance on her two closest advisors, Nick Timothy and Fiona Hill. Both earned a poor reputation as being May's 'guard dogs' and both had too much influence. Neither were elected to anything and as the inquests got underway, they were accused of inserting elements into the manifesto that had not been agreed at Cabinet level or by the party as a whole. This was denied by Timothy but it is what happens when a Prime Minister is surrounded by unelected advisors and to the near-exclusion of everybody else – it happened with Tony Blair, it happened with David Cameron and it happens with Jeremy Corbyn (especially with Jeremy Corbyn).

Curiously, May had another close advisor, one Oliver Robbins. Robbins is a civil servant, not an elected MP and is widely seen as the prime 'behind-the-scenes' mover over the weakening and watering-down of the UK's Brexit negotiations as he is also noted for being an enthusiastic backer of the EU. Why is he involved? As somebody who has not been granted his position by the people, he is as his title says; a civil servant. His job is to do just that, serve the people and not try to alter the will of the majority.

Oliver Robbins and those like him should not – indeed, must not – be allowed to rule over the population they are supposed to serve.

A second answer is that the Conservatives have had a habit of taking for granted that more mature voters would vote for them rather than Labour, which is not entirely true but does have some precedent to it. The manifesto elements that caused the biggest rifts were those that appeared to adversely affect older members of society, the very people upon whom the Conservatives have traditionally relied. *'An ageing population…'* Discard them at your peril for everybody is going there (unless…Logan's Run…).

May's third big mistake was in having her name plastered over everything. David Cameron tried this once, at a bye-election, with the ballot papers giving the correct party names except for one which read, 'David Cameron's Conservatives'. The bye-election result was disastrous and putting the party leader's name above and beyond everything was not tried again – until 2017. The UK does not elect a President; it elects a party by voting for its MPs, not for a personality leader. Granted the public perception of a party leader does help but it is not 'the' defining characteristic.

The Conservatives were also guilty of assuming that the substantial number of people who voted for UKIP at the 2015 election were all disaffected Tories. Yet UKIP themselves had made a big deal out of the fact that they were taking votes from both Conservative and Labour. With Brexit underway, the arrogant assumption that all would flock to the Conservatives was nothing short of sheer negligence, as was the equally arrogant assumption that all older voters would automatically vote Conservative.

There was however, another factor at work in 2017. Despite the wedge driven between generations written of earlier in this book, if there is one thing that Jeremy Corbyn has done brilliantly well – and just maybe doing the country an inestimably great service by so doing – it has been to prove that young people really don't care what a Prime Minister looks like. The Blair legacy of being young, cool and funky is dead and will not rise again unless it is allowed to.

Jeremy Corbyn is an older man. He has thinning grey hair. He has a grey beard. He has wrinkles. He is (almost) everybody's favourite Granddad - but the young voted for him and in substantial numbers. This is where personality does come in, where how one comes across is a part of things. Theresa May was shockingly badly advised. At no time did she separate herself as a person from Corbyn. At no time did she say things like, 'I don't do hugging, It's not my persona to go around being emotional. Yes, I'm comfortable with who I am and I like to wear clothes that I'm comfortable in. But don't expect me to be who I'm not.' May's campaigning was marked for its 'put-up' look, it's stage-managed appearance.

Corbyn on the other hand, seemed quite comfortable chatting to anybody. Including the first-time voter, the ones who had not been able to vote in the Brexit referendum as well as those slightly older.

Plebiscite

He was also ruthless in his pursuance of them, particularly in promises to get rid of University fees. Not only that, but those behind him were also adept at using social media, and they did so to great effect. Why did the Tories not have somebody doing the same?

Because those who ran the campaign simply assumed. They simply assumed that there were enough people with long memories who would remember Corbyn's past associations with terrorist organisations. They simply assumed that the publicity accorded to that aspect of Jeremy Corbyn would be believed and not put down to unpleasant sniping on the part of right-wing media. They simply assumed that all those traditional voters would just turn up and back them. They didn't - which is why younger voters had such an impact. There has been a tendency for a significant number of 18-25 year-olds not voting and of those that have taken an active interest in politics, many have swung towards socialism before growing a little older and turning away from it. This is because they have never owned anything. They have never had to be responsible for anything, like paying for their own home, like bringing up a family and realising that they have to make ends meet. The left-wing influence on the young today is however, greater than it has ever been, thanks to the ideology that is stuffed into them at school and then University. Ask yourself something; how many people went to University before 1997? How many people go to University now? What happened in 1997? Answer – Blair. The Blair Government embarked on a massive programme of University expansion. What had been technical Colleges and similar further education establishments became 'Universities' instead. Attendance at these new Universities shot up. To pay for it, Blair's New Labour introduced tuition fees…

No, not the evil Tories – Labour.

Now, in 2017, Labour are saying they will drop them. How all these universities will be then paid for is a little less clear but it has always been the Conservatives who cleared up the economic mess left by a Labour term of office in Government.

But that doesn't matter! That the ruinous finances left behind after an unprecedented thirteen years of Labour profligacy (they had never been in Government for that long before) doesn't matter either! Uncle Jezza can sort it all out! He's cute and cuddly.

Did Jeremy Corbyn really expect to win the general election of 2017? Yes, he campaigned to win, of course - but did he, deep in his heart of hearts, really believe he would? Or did it suit his purpose to be Leader of a party that could oppose everything, promise even more and never actually have to worry about paying for it? Or of having the responsibility for everything?

Only he can tell you that.

One final example of the Labour party's current way of thinking;

The MP for Tottenham in North London is David Lammy. Following former footballer and current sports presenter Gary Lineker's avowed opposition to Brexit and an interview on Sky news in which Lineker reiterated his view, Lammy posted a tweet on the subject, in which he wrote:

> 'Top man Gary Lineker. I'm biased he did play for Spurs but thank god some people are prepared to stick their neck out and not pander to the "will of the people" bollocks'.

The will of the people bollocks?

My question to David Lammy MP is therefore, a very simple one - what about the will of the people who gave you your job to start with?

The reality however, is that in 2017, and as time moved on and in to 2018, those behind Jeremy Corbyn can sense that, for the very first time in the history of the United Kingdom, an extreme, far-left socialist government could be a reality.

.

17 Re-run

*Because if you can prove you're a victim, all rules are off. You can lash
out at people. You don't have to be accountable for anything.*

Brandon Stanton

People became fed up with Brexit. There is no doubt at all that, since
the referendum on UK membership was held, a vast majority of the
country's population simply wanted the on-going furore to end and
for Parliament, along with its members, to get on with it, including
significant numbers who voted to stay but accept that they lost and
the will of the majority must be carried out (one can reasonably
suggest that remain voters who do are the majority in this respect
also). Yet three years on, the UK has not left. Why not?

Put simply, the UK is still in the EU because of the way in which
matters have been dealt with. Or not dealt with, depending on how
one looks at it. With the result of the referendum known, there was
much trumpeting from leading figures on the leave side that a trade
deal would be done and the UK now had a bright future free of the
shackles of EU bureaucracy and diktat. There was however, just one
small problem in the way - the EU itself. More correctly, those same
highly-paid and unelected bureaucrats presented their own barrier.

The EU, as an organisation is a profoundly undemocratic one.
Whilst it may well have an elected parliament that, to most people,
seems to be in charge, in fact the EU is run by the EU Commission,
not the parliament. It is the Commission that runs things with the
parliament being more of a rubber-stamping talking shop. Its
presence is mere window-dressing.

The EU is also notorious for conceding that referendums will be
held from time to time within the countries that are members of it,
but on each and every occasion that a referendum has been held,
when the result has gone against the EU, it has machinated,
obfuscated and indulged in subtle rewording to ensure that another
is held and the 'right' result is acquired.

Denmark held a referendum in 1992 over the Maastricht Treaty
with a very narrow vote against. A year later, a second was held and
this time voted for, with 56.7% of those voting in favour, with a
turnout of 86.5%.

In 2008, Irish voters rejected the Treaty of Lisbon but in 2009, voted
in favour after the European Council and the Irish Government
released separate documents, referred to as the 'Irish Guarantees',
that persuaded 67.1% to vote in favour, although the turnout was

only 59.0% of those eligible to vote.

The most infamous was the referendum in Greece over the bailout conditions imposed on the Greek government's debt crisis. A majority of the voters rejected the bailout conditions. However, shortly afterwards the government accepted a bailout with even harsher conditions than the ones rejected by the voters – which rather rendered the exercise of holding a referendum to begin with somewhat pointless.

This was the biggest question over the UK's vote in 2016. The question on the UK's ballot papers was a very simple one:

> Should the United Kingdom remain a member of the European Union or leave the European Union?

There is nothing complicated about the question. However, what made it so was the status of the referendum itself. This is an extract from the European Union Referendum Bill 2015-16:

5 Types of referendum

This Bill requires a referendum to be held on the question of the UK's continued membership of the European Union (EU) before the end of 2017. It does not contain any requirement for the UK Government to implement the results of the referendum, nor set a time limit by which a vote to leave the EU should be implemented. Instead, this is a type of referendum known as pre-legislative or consultative, which enables the electorate to voice an opinion which then influences the Government in its policy decisions. The referendums held in Scotland, Wales and Northern Ireland in 1997 and 1998 are examples of this type, where opinion was tested before legislation was introduced. The UK does not have constitutional provisions which would require the results of a referendum to be implemented, unlike, for example, the Republic of Ireland, where the circumstances in which a binding referendum should be held are set out in its constitution. In contrast, the legislation which provided for the referendum held on AV in May 2011 would have implemented the new system of voting without further legislation, provided that the boundary changes also provided for in the Parliamentary Voting System and Constituency Act 2011 were also implemented. In the event, there was a substantial majority against any change. The 1975 referendum was held after the re-negotiated terms of the UK's EC membership had been agreed by all EC Member States and the terms set out in a command paper and agreed by both Houses.

Re-run

So what does this actually mean?

It depends on how you look at it. Take for example the following two quotes, one from a dedicated remainer and one from and equally dedicated leaver:

> The referendum was an advisory referendum
> *Dominic Grieve MP, 10 October 2016.*

> This was not an advisory referendum
> *John Redwood MP, 7 November, 2016.*

If one accepts that, since the UK does not actually have a written constitution and referendums simply test public opinion, then it could be said there is no point in having one if the result is ignored.

However, the argument now moves from a legal one to a political one; then Prime Minister David Cameron and numerous others, from all parties, said that the British people would make the decision. The leaflet sent out by Cameron's government said:

> This is your decision. The Government will implement what you decide.

That sounds rather straightforward. The same commitment was made by the Labour party and everybody else. It is this that has caused the problems since.

A significant number of MPs, as has already been stated earlier, have reneged on that commitment – and people are rather upset about it. It is why a number of MPs currently sitting will not be when the results of the next general election come along (which could be sooner than anticipated).

The result of 2016 was widely expected to be heavily in favour of remaining. So detached have the political classes become that any other result was never considered, hence the metaphorical earthquake that reverberated around Westminster when that narrow majority for leaving was announced. The immediate fallout was the departure of David Cameron and the coronation of Theresa May as Prime Minister.

The pronouncements from various members of her government that a great trade deal would be negotiated with the EU was then stymied by the EU Commission, who refused to even begin discussion over trade or anything else until a withdrawal agreement had been concluded.

My remarks earlier in this book were originally written (as I said) to begin with some time before the referendum had even been thought of. I further commented (on pages 59-60) how essentially simple it all should be but pointed out that there would be those who wished to obstruct things and by insisting on a withdrawal agreement first, the EU Commission put a spoke in the wheels of the UK's departure.

Of itself the concept of an agreement over the terms of the departure is not actually unfair. However, the terms contained within it, terms included at the insistence of the EU Commission's negotiators (who proved far more cunning than those from Theresa May's side), made the agreement that was concluded unpalatable from the point of view of many MPs who were on the side of leave. The most notable was the Irish 'backstop' that, in effect, kept Northern Ireland in the EU and excluded it from the rest of the UK. There are, or perhaps now were, other aspects that have been shown to heavily in favour the EU. All of which meant that when it came to voting the agreement through parliament it was defeated three times.

Obviously remain favouring MPs would not vote for it but the involvement of leave MPs voting against it as well led, ultimately, to Theresa May's fall as Prime Minster.

Yet it was – still – not all this that has been one of the primary causes of the hysteria over leaving the EU. Lost among all the extravagant verbosity was the true meaning of the withdrawal agreement. The howling from the rooftops and soapboxes over 'the deal' masked what it really was; an agreement over the terms of leaving the EU, and paving the way for what would replace it – the trade agreement that would then be negotiated between the UK and the EU. Once that had been done, the withdrawal agreement, including the backstop, would have been superseded - but so many people now have confused 'the deal' with not having a withdrawal agreement – 'no deal'. This includes politicians, who also rant on about 'no deal' as if it is some kind of panacea for all ills, and those on the other side who screech 'no deal' is unacceptable - we must have a 'deal'.

A 'deal' over…what?

None have been able to really articulate what they are on about. You can count on one hand the numbers of British politicians, and for that matter business people as well, who have been really accurate with what they say about having a deal or not having a deal.

For significant numbers of ordinary people, deal or no deal has become the be-all and end-all of everything. Twitter users have gone ballistic over 'just walking away' with no deal.

The withdrawal agreement was just that - nothing more. It was probably one of the most imperfect documents ever devised and there is little doubt that the EU Commission was at its best in the way it out-thought and outplayed Theresa May and those around her. But it was still only an agreement on the terms of leaving.

Re-run

It would still have been replaced by a subsequent trade agreement, one that would have dealt with the abilities of people to move from EU countries to the UK and vice-versa; one that would have enabled business to go on and pretty much as it has done for the more than four decades the UK has been in the EU (and as it did before the UK joined). It is that 'deal' that counts.

For all those who have espoused the idea of walking away with 'no deal', what might be the result? That's hard to say, especially since the EU and the UK have already signed agreements in any number of areas that will allow things to carry on, like flying to Spain for a holiday – an activity much loved by so many in the UK and the Spanish would not take too kindly to losing the UK's business (just remember to take your passport when you go...).

The continual scare-mongering over 'crashing out' had gone beyond farcical, as were the demands to 'just leave'. Departing the EU was always going to involve compromise somewhere and the inflexible attitude of both sides was absurd. Go back to pages 59 and 60 again – I solved the Brexit crisis already.

With the departure of Theresa May, obviously the party that gained enough seats in the House of Commons at the last election to form a government needed a new leader; hence it followed the same process as has been the case in times past when a Prime Minister left office in between general elections and the Conservatives elected Boris Johnson. Having done so, as party leader, he became (as of autumn 2019) Prime Minister.

Again there were screams of anguish from Labour (and others) over the legitimacy of Prime Minister Johnson but there wasn't a peep out of them when Gordon Brown replaced Tony Blair. Sorry folks but you can't have it both ways. If it was okay for Gordon to nip in to replace Tony and if it was okay for Jim Callaghan to take over from Harold Wilson then it is okay for Boris to replace Theresa.

So why was Labour so upset? Was it because Boris Johnson, for all his undoubted flaws, had 'people-power'? In the few short weeks since he became PM, the Tories took a significant lead over Labour in polls. Such polls have been shown to be startlingly inaccurate when it comes to general elections and there can be little doubt that Boris Johnson has been more popular than Jeremy Corbyn, whose own flaws were increasingly exposed as time had moved on. But the UK was not at a general election – yet. By October 2019 that could change however, because Johnson, in effect, staked his leadership on taking the UK out of the EU – as *all* politicians promised to do in 2016.

Love him or loath him Johnson made an impressive start, sweeping out the old guard in his government and replacing them with a very new look. He announced some impressive policies also, many of which struck a chord with people around the UK.

The relationship between the UK and the EU however, has proved to be a thorn in the side of the Conservatives since the country joined. Edward Heath, while Tory PM, took the UK in to it (and without a referendum), Margaret Thatcher was famously at odds with it, John Major fell because of it, at least in part, and it did for David Cameron as well.

So Boris Johnson wants to take the UK out of it; 'do or die' as he said. Yet Members of Parliament (elected by you, the ones whose boss you are, remember) still conspired to frustrate both him and the majority of people who voted for leave. Some of these MPs, from all sides of the house, conspired to grab power from the government of Theresa May and impose their own version on the UK.

That was and never has been the job of an MP, any MP, of any party. Whether it is right or wrong (and this is a debate for another time), who becomes a member of the government is in the hands of the party that gets enough seats to have the right to form it, in this case the Conservatives. Thus it is the party's leader who becomes Prime Minister and it is the PM who decides who to appoint as a member of the government.

For other MPs to seize power – or attempt to – is little more than a coup. Yet as these words are written and this version of the book goes into the print process, the word 'coup' has been hurled at the Prime Minister as he prorogued parliament – in other words, suspended it.

Johnson did so because, as he and his government said, the house had been sitting for longer than at any time in living memory and as a new government with new policies (which it is), the PM wants a Queen's Speech to introduce new legislation. Johnson stands accused of denying democracy and all manner of similar things but...by doing so now, at the end of August, parliament would be suspended anyway due to the party conferences held at this time of year. Given the dates announced by Johnson, just four extra days will be lost to parliament - hardly a coup or an affront to democracy.

That aside, Prime Ministers have always prorogued parliament and for various reasons. Why the hysteria in 2019? Is it the last desperate throw of remain activism? That is for you to decide – as you will should there be a general election over the departure of the UK from the EU. Johnson has at least, shown some spirit, some dynamism; some leadership and some individuality. For far too long the UK has had bland, dull and rather insipid politicians, people who have never lived as ordinary people do. Boris Johnson will stand on what he achieves or fall on what he doesn't.

Remember however, and with regard to the rest of them, bad politicians are elected by people who don't vote.

·

18 Linguistica Acrobatica

Who are we without our words?

Melina Marchetta

Language is a fascinating thing. As you may have noticed, I sometimes pay little attention to technically perfect grammar when writing books (even one such as this which does have a serious theme to it). I do so because reading can either be a strenuous effort or a relaxing way of spending time, while at the same time informing, entertaining, educating and provoking. If you have got this far, then it might be fair to suggest that I've done okay (even if you disagree vehemently with every word).

Language, its use, meaning, interpretation, in fact everything connected with it and especially in the written word, could and should be a reflection on the world around it. Grammar does have a purpose and a place even so. What grammar does is put structure around what we say and write, the idea being that anybody and everybody can understand what is being said and there are those who stick to perfect grammar rigidly. However, when perfect grammar is used to the exclusion of anything and everything else, it can result in wooden and stilted speech – and writing.

There are greater writers and authors than I, so on the basis of learning from them, as Kingsley Amis put it:

> And the idea that *and* must not begin a sentence, or even a paragraph, is an empty superstition. The same goes for *but*. Indeed either word can give unimprovably early warning of the sort of thing that is to follow.'
> (from *'The King's English / 1997*).

Commentator Peter Hitchens has described the English language as a 'beautiful, flexible, living architecture' and he was right. So the slavish adherence to perfect grammar so beloved of by some book publishers and others could be said to be unnecessary. This in fact, is not so. Grammar is important and it is equally important to know when and how to use it – and when not to.

What makes language so fascinating though, are the differences between nations that speak the same one. Probably the most infamous is that of UK English and American English. Such are the differences in spelling, pronunciation and interpretation that Winston Churchill once said that the United Kingdom and the USA were two nations separated only by a common language. The two countries however, get along quite well and don't generally have too much of an issue over deciphering what one says to the other.

It gets a little trickier however, when English is not the first language of somebody who moves to the UK and has to learn to speak it. If one goes to live and work in France it makes perfect sense to learn how to speak French, which is an undeniably beautiful language. Indeed, the average French citizen would probably insist that you do. Yet in the UK, we have become very lax in being equally insistent. That laxity has led to social division and inequality where it need not have done. It has led to people reacting violently when faced with something (or somebody) that they do not understand. There are significantly large numbers of people in the UK that do not have the correct understanding of words and their true meaning. Born, bred, raised and educated in the UK, and with English as their only language, some people, because of their lack of education, do not know how to respond properly to whatever it may be that they are faced with.

More importantly, the lack of linguistic skills, either from those with English as their first language or from those who have had to learn it (if they do), has led to unneeded suffering, particularly in the NHS, where poor communication has had tragic results. Yet English is the most widely spoken language in the world (which also has the side effect of making UK citizens rather lazy when it comes to learning another language – shame upon you, although not me since I do speak a second language; far from perfectly but I can get by).

Despite the potential for disaster, not being entirely fluent in any language can have its amusing side. The German word for Cake is very similar to the word used to describe the facility, the room, where all foods are cooked and prepared and my father's second wife, who spoke German quite well, nevertheless got it slightly wrong and once asked a waiter if his restaurant had any kitchens.

Some of what follows have their roots in the writers not having English as their first language, some don't. You can fathom out for yourself which may be which but these are sentences exactly as typed by NHS Medical Secretaries (with thanks to Paul F. who found them and shared them on Facebook);

1.   The patient has no previous history of suicide.
2.   Patient has left her white blood cells at another hospital.
3.   Patient's medical history has been remarkably insignificant, with only a 40 pound weight gain in the past three days.
4.   She has no rigours or shaking chills, but her husband states she was very hot in bed last night.
5.   Patient has chest pain if she lies on her left side for over a year.

Linguistica Acrobatica

6.   On the second day the knee was better and on the third day it disappeared.

7.   The patient is tearful and crying constantly. She also appears to be depressed.

8.   The patient has been depressed since she began seeing me in 1993.

9.   Discharge status: Alive, but without my permission.

10.   Healthy appearing decrepit 69-year old male, mentally alert, but forgetful.

11.   Patient had cereal for breakfast and anorexia for lunch.

12.   She is numb from her toes down.

13.   While in ER, she was examined, x-rated and sent home.

14.   The skin was moist and dry.

15.   Occasional, constant, infrequent headaches.

16.   Patient was alert and unresponsive.

17.   Rectal examination revealed a normal size thyroid.

18.   She stated that she had been constipated for most of her life until she got a divorce.

19.   I saw your patient today, who is still under our care for physical therapy.

20.   Both breasts are equal and reactive to light and accommodation.

21.   Examination of genitalia reveals that he is circus-sized.

22.   The lab test indicated abnormal lover function.

23.   Skin: somewhat pale, but present.

24.   The pelvic exam will be done later on the floor.

25.   Large brown stool ambulating in the hall.

26.   Patient has two teenage children, but no other abnormalities.

27.   When she fainted, her eyes rolled around the room.

28.   The patient was in his usual state of good health until his aeroplane ran out of fuel and crashed.

29.   Between you and me, we ought to be able to get this lady pregnant.

30.   She slipped on the ice and apparently her legs went in separate directions in early December.

31.   Patient was seen in consultation by Dr. Smith, who felt we should sit on the abdomen and I agree.

32.   The patient was to have a bowel resection. However, he took a job as a stockbroker instead.

33.   By the time he was admitted, his rapid heart had stopped, and he was feeling better.

Why do so many people want to come to the UK, to Britain? Britain may have been, or even still be, a nation of shopkeepers but it is also a nation of little empire builders who don't like the idea that somebody else might be right, be better and that somebody else might succeed. And the United Kingdom is a country...

Where little children of three are told to sign a behaviour agreement saying they will not use homophobic or racist words...
Where little children of five, seven or nine years old become sex offenders...
Where all men are automatically terrorists or paedophiles...
Where registered sex offenders are asked by their supervising Police Officers what they think about whilst masturbating (really – I promise you I'm not making that up)...
Where state control continues to wrap it's tentacles around everything and everybody...
Where people are encouraged to spy on each other and report their observations to an over-mighty police service that thinks it is and has become a police force...
Where free speech is under threat like never before...
Where significant - and rising - numbers cannot afford to have a home, rented or otherwise, because having a home costs too much...
Where the old are nothing more than a nuisance (Logan's Run is coming)...
And more...and worse...

Points to remember:

'Free' does not actually mean free
You are not entitled to someone else's hard-earned money. Ever
You cannot tax a nation into health and prosperity
'The Rich' are not responsible for your financial situation. You are.
More Government means less freedom. ALWAYS!

One final quote...and to avoid any accusations of gender bias, the following was said by a woman:

> 'Let me give you my vision:
> A man's right to work as he will, to spend what he earns, to own property, to have the state as servant and not as master - these are the British inheritance. They are the essence of a free economy....and on that freedom all others depend'.

Margaret Thatcher.
October 10, 1975.

■

19 Zed Carr's Happiness Maxims

I really hope the zombie apocalypse doesn't happen while I'm in bed asleep. The last thing I want is to spend eternity walking the earth naked and undead.

Sam Goldstone Harris

1. 'Move your body.'
2. 'Eat right.'
3. 'Step out of your comfort zone.'
4. 'Be open-minded.'
5. 'Be optimistic.'
6. 'Forgive yourself.'
7. 'Laugh more.'
8. 'Never stop learning...but realise you'll never know everything.'
9. 'Stop comparing yourself with others.'
10. 'Do some crazy shit.'
11. 'Take charge of your cash.'
12. 'Enjoy animals and wildlife.'
13. 'Think in the now and Experience in the now – Be mindful.'
14. 'Give to worthy causes (not just the first guy rattling a tin).'
15. 'Find a job you love.'
16. 'Share your joy.'
17. 'Limit social media use.'
18. 'Don't take yourself too seriously.'
19. 'Multi-define yourself.'
20. 'Be happy to say 'no'.'
21. 'Trust yourself.'
22. 'Love yourself.'
23. 'Respect yourself.'
24. 'Break with convention.'
25. 'Don't be afraid to fail.'
26. 'Avoid negative people and liars.'
27. 'Forgive everyone, especially your family and friends – everyone screws up and most people live in their own delusions, one way or another...'

Comments of a Common Man

28. 'Live a 'quality' frugal life. Good quality clothes, belongings etc..'
29. 'Do what really works for you.'
30. 'Give up good for great – invest in yourself.'
31. 'Don't sweat the small stuff.'
32. 'Embrace the arts; art, music, drama, dance, poetry, literature, architecture.'
33. 'Grow things.'
34. 'Be creative artistically.'
35. 'Help others.'
36. 'Take an interest in local issues.'
37. 'Always remain within touching distance of 'home'.'
38. 'Learn to cook.'
39. 'Have plenty of sun and sea (which makes everyone happy!)'
40. 'Learn new skills (languages, musical instruments, car maintenance…etc)'
41. 'Ditch perfectionism – it's a disgusting habit.'
42. 'Always look for the good thing in what may seem like a bad thing.'
43. 'Be persistent – Don't give up.'
44. 'Pamper yourself, on occasion.'
45. 'Take ownership of every square inch of your body.'
46. 'Remember the past but live in the present.'
47. 'Know yourself.'
48. 'Just do it!'
49. 'Have fun!'

I would add another two to that already impressive list:

50. Take responsibility. Of yourself, for yourself and most of all, of your Government; hold it and those within it to account.
51. Accept the risk and pay the price of freedom.

Because if you don't you cease to be free.

.